THE SOLAR SYSTEM

CONNECTING STUDENTS TO SCIENCE SERIES

By
DON POWERS, Ph.D., and JOHN B. BEAVER, Ph.D.

COPYRIGHT © 2004 Mark Twain Media, Inc.

ISBN 1-58037-278-3

Printing No. CD-404005

Mark Twain Media, Inc., Publishers
Distributed by Carson-Dellosa Publishing Company, Inc.

TABLE OF CONTENTS

INTRODUCTION TO THE SERIES

The Connecting Students to Science Series is designed for grades 5–8+. This series will introduce the following topics: Simple Machines, Electricity and Magnetism, Rocks and Minerals, Atmosphere and Weather, Chemistry, Light and Color, The Solar System, and Sound. Each book will contain an introduction to the topic, naive concepts, inquiry activities, content integration, materials lists, children's literature connections, curriculum resources, assessment documents, and a bibliography. Students will develop an understanding of the concepts and processes of science through the use of good scientific techniques. Students will be engaged in higher-level thinking skills while doing fun and interesting activities. All of the activities will be aligned with the National Science Education Standards and National Council of Teachers of Mathematics Standards.

This series is written for classroom teachers, parents, families, and students. The books in this series can be used as a full unit of study or as individual lessons to supplement existing textbooks or curriculum programs. Activities are designed to be pedagogically sound, hands-on, minds-on science activities that support the National Science Education Standards (NSES). Parents and students can use this series as an enhancement to what is being done in the classroom or as a tutorial at home.

The procedures and content background are clearly explained in the introduction and within the individual activities. Materials used in the activities are commonly found in classrooms and homes.

HISTORICAL PERSPECTIVES OF THE SOLAR SYSTEM (CONT.)

Knowledge of the solar system has been developing since the beginning of mankind. Ancient civilizations would look toward the sky to explain various natural phenomena. As they observed and studied the sky, they began to record their observations. As their observations were studied, they discovered that many of their observations followed predictable cycles. The sun rose and set as they predicted; stars moved across the sky as they predicted. At the same time, they discovered that some objects in the sky were more unpredictable and appeared to wander across the sky without regard to the motion of the sun and stars. These "wanderers" were later named planets.

Living without the aid of telescopes, the ancient observers could only see five of the planets: Mercury, Venus, Mars, Jupiter, and Saturn. After observing these naked-eye planets for many years, patterns of motion began to appear. As these patterns became more recognizable, man began to formulate explanations for these movements. As time passed, these explanations have been modified and refined. One of the earliest explanations was proposed in the first century by Ptolemy and involved eight different spheres—one for each of the five planets plus one each for the sun, the moon, and the stars, with the earth at the center. While this was a complicated explanation, it was widely accepted because of its earth-centered basis and because the thought of ever leaving the earth was nonexistent.

In the early 1500s, Nicholas Copernicus proposed a simpler explanation of the motions of the sun, moon, planets, and stars. In the Copernican model, the sun was at the center, while the planets, earth, moon, and stars revolved around the sun. Copernicus's explanation was not accepted by the scholars of the world until about 100 years later when works by Johannes Kepler and Galileo Galilei were published. Kepler viewed the Copernican Theory as being in error because, according to Kepler, the orbits of the moving bodies were elliptical and not circular. Because of Galileo's outspokenness in regards to his model that placed the sun, and not the earth, at the center of all motion, the Catholic Church excommunicated him and placed him under house arrest until his death. It was not until the 1990s that Pope John Paul II, on behalf of the Catholic Church, forgave Galileo and stated that his model of the solar system was not in conflict with the teachings of the Church.

Our knowledge of the solar system continued to progress with the development of the telescope. Again it was Galileo who first pointed his crude telescope toward Jupiter and observed the movement of four moons—Io, Callisto, Ganymede, and Europa—around the giant gaseous planet. Since that time, as many as 16 moons have been discovered to orbit Jupiter. In the book *Seeing and Believing,* Richard Panek describes Galileo's early experiences with the telescope. How exciting it must have been to discover mountains, valleys, and plains on the

HISTORICAL PERSPECTIVES OF THE SOLAR SYSTEM (CONT.)

moon and to observe the orbs of light that moved relative to the planet Jupiter! Panek describes Galileo's experiences in the following sentences. "He had to struggle against the breath that clouded the glass, against the blood that shook the hand that steadied the (telescope) tube. The more he searched, the more he found." (Panek, 1998, p. 12). It is not difficult to imagine yourself in the shoes of Galileo making these early discoveries.

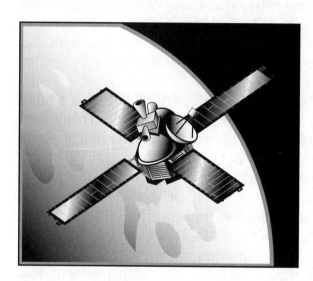

Our knowledge of the solar system has come not only from the use of the telescope. Man himself has ventured into the unknown regions by landing and walking on the moon in July 1969. While humans have ventured no farther than the moon, they have used observational tools to travel to other planets. In 1974 and 1975, the United States' *Mariner 10* spacecraft repeatedly orbited the planet Mercury, photographing the surface of the nearest planet to the sun. The atmosphere of the earth's nearest neighbor, Venus, has prevented observers on Earth from seeing its surface. However in 1993, the *Magellan* spacecraft with the use of radar was able to view the Venusian landscape, revealing it as a desolate planet with a liquid atmosphere of carbon dioxide surrounding it. In 1997, the United States safely landed the unmanned vehicle *Sojourner* on the planet Mars, and the Mars Rover explored the surface of the planet and transmitted data and pictures back to the earth.

Ongoing research continues to reveal new discoveries about our solar system and beyond. *Voyager* missions have flown past Jupiter, Saturn, and Uranus and continue on towards the outer boundaries of the solar system and beyond. New discoveries in these far-reaching areas are continually announced by NASA, the Jet Propulsion Laboratory, and other agencies. With continued research, discoveries may be made in regard to possible intelligent life elsewhere in the universe. One of the most exciting projects in astronomy is the Hubble Deep Field Telescope. It was launched on April 25, 1990, from the space shuttle *Discovery* (STS-31). The Hubble Telescope has gathered information from the deepest reaches of space. It is expected to gather data for twenty years through 2010, when it will be shut down and returned to Earth. Information about the Hubble Deep Field Project can be found online at www.hubblesite.org.

Movement of the Sun, the Earth, and the Moon

The movements of the earth, sun, and moon are probably the most observed phenomena in the solar system. The earth revolves around the sun once every 365.25 days. The completion of this revolution represents the passing of one year. The usual calendar year is 365 days in length, but every fourth year, a leap year, which is 366 days, is observed in order to make up for the one-fourth of a day each year. The earth also rotates once on its axis every 23 hours and 56 minutes. This rotational motion results in the passage of one day, or 24 hours on

HISTORICAL PERSPECTIVES OF THE SOLAR SYSTEM (CONT.)

our clocks. The earth's axis of rotation is not parallel to the sun but is tilted at a 23.5 degree angle. The axis of rotation runs from the North Pole to the South Pole, through the center of the earth. The North Pole is always pointing in the direction of Polaris, the North Star. As a result, the North Pole is generally pointing in the direction of the sun during the summer months in the Northern Hemisphere and generally away from the sun during the winter months of the year. This tilt results in different portions of the earth receiving differing amounts of sunlight during the year, depending on where Earth is in its orbit of the sun. This causes the earth to have four major seasons each year: summer, fall, winter, and spring. The varying amounts of sunlight also cause the earth to be heated unevenly and results in various kinds of weather and climates around the world.

As the earth is traveling around the sun, the earth is also being orbited by a natural satellite, the moon. It takes the moon 27.3 days to revolve once around the earth. This is also the length of time it takes the moon to rotate once on its axis. This results in observers on Earth seeing the same side of the moon all of the time. The movement of the moon around the earth

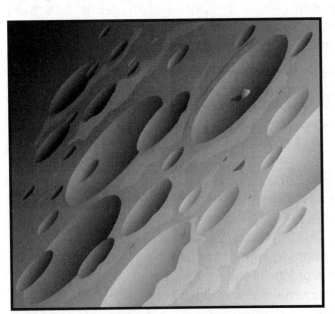

and the earth's movement around the sun result in a change in the portion of the moon that is reflecting sunlight. This is referred to as the moon's phases. The four major phases of the moon are: new moon, first quarter moon, full moon, and third (or last) quarter moon. Additional phases of the moon are identified according to whether the phase is a crescent moon, where less than one-half of the visible surface is illuminated; or a gibbous moon, which is when more than one-half the visible surface is illuminated. These intermediary phases may also be classified as either a waxing moon (i.e., waxing crescent or waxing gibbous) if the visible surface of the moon is increasing in size, or a waning moon if the visible surface of the moon is decreasing in size. The complete cycle following a new moon is: waxing crescent, first quarter, waxing gibbous, full moon, waning gibbous, third quarter, waning crescent, and new moon. The moon phases repeat themselves every 29.5 days or about once a month. Occasionally, there will be a full moon twice in one month; when this happens, the second full moon is called a "blue moon."

While several theories exist as to the formation of the moon, one of the most popular assumes that a large unknown object struck the earth many years ago, blasting material away from the earth. This material was captured in the earth's gravitational orbit, thus forming the moon. Pieces of this debris collided with each other, causing enough heat to melt and fuse the particles together, eventually forming the moon. Since its initial formation, the moon has cooled and been bombarded by millions of pieces of other space debris to create the cratered surface that is now observed on the moon. The mountains on the moon were formed through geological

4

HISTORICAL PERSPECTIVES OF THE SOLAR SYSTEM (CONT.)

activity during the moon's initial formation when the moon was hot and supported lava flows and other mountain-building forces. Because the moon has no atmosphere, wind, water, or other erosional forces, the impact of space debris creates features that remain unchanged through time. In July 1969, the United States *Apollo 11* spacecraft landed on the moon, and Neil Armstrong and Edwin Aldrin became the first persons to ever walk on the moon. The footprints left during the *Apollo 11* and the subsequent three expeditions to the moon's surface will remain unchanged on the surface until they are altered by later space debris impacts. The four *Apollo* missions that actually landed on the moon's surface included *Apollo 11* in July 1969, *Apollo 15* in July 1971, *Apollo 16* in April 1972, and *Apollo 17* in December 1972. Eugene Cernan was the last *Apollo* astronaut to walk on the moon on December 14, 1972. He was accompanied by Harrison Schmitt, the only geologist to have visited the moon. Complete details on the entire *Apollo* space program can be found online at: www.nasa.edu/apollo/apollo.htm.

Planets

The most popular scientific theory explaining the formation of the planets involves the "Big Bang Theory." According to this theory, many years ago, a huge explosion occurred that sent space debris throughout the universe. Clusters of this debris formed stars such as our sun. According to current research, our sun was formed as a rotating ball of gas in the center of a large cloud of interstellar gas and dust. As this cloud of gas and dust continued to spin, dust particles collided with each other and eventually formed small protoplanets. These protoplanets continued to collide and collect dust particles until planets orbiting in the same direction around the sun were created. Nine planets and one asteroid belt make up the known solar system. The planets are, in order from the sun, Mercury, Venus, Earth, Mars, Jupiter, Saturn, Uranus, Neptune, and Pluto.

The asteroid belt, a collection of thousands of rocky masses, is located between the orbits of Mars and Jupiter. The largest of the asteroids in this group are Ceres, Pallas, and Vesta. Ceres has a diameter of about 600 miles (950 km); Pallas and Vesta have diameters of about 340 miles (550 km). Scientists have identified about 120 other asteroids with diameters larger than 120 miles (200 km) orbiting with Ceres, Pallas, and Vesta. The remaining asteroids are less than 120 miles in diameter, but most are over 1/2 mile (1 km) across. Some books refer to the asteroids as planetoids.

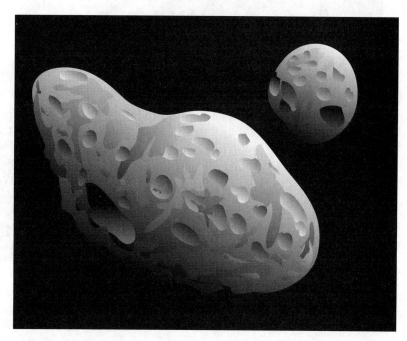

HISTORICAL PERSPECTIVES OF THE SOLAR SYSTEM (CONT.)

The position of the planets in the solar system causes them to have unique physical features. The first four planets in the solar system, Mercury, Venus, Earth, and Mars, are referred to as the **inner belt,** or **terrestrial,** planets. Mercury and Venus, due to their closeness to the sun, are very hot and unsuitable for habitation. The earth's position in the solar system is unique, in that it is the only planet that can support life as we know it. Mars, or the "Red Planet," would appear to be most amenable to supporting some form of life, but no solid evidence of life, past or present, has been discovered through observations of the planet. The inner belt of planets is separated from the outer belt of planets by the asteroid belt. The outer belt includes the Jovian Planets: Jupiter, Saturn, Uranus, and Neptune. They are different from the terrestrial planets in that they have no solid surface. These large gas giants are surrounded by gaseous clouds that get thicker closer to the center of the planet. The most distant planet of our solar system, Pluto, is a cold, dense planet about which little is known. Pluto is smaller than Earth's moon and only twice the size of its own moon, Charon. Pluto's orbit is quite eccentric relative to the other planets. Its orbit takes it far above and below the orbits of the other planets. Additionally, its orbit intersects that of Neptune's from time to time. The last time this occurred was between the years 1979 and 1999. During this twenty-year period, Neptune was farther away from the sun than Pluto.

NAIVE IDEAS AND SOLAR SYSTEM CONCEPTS AND FACTS

The naive ideas described below are misconceptions that students may have about the solar system.

Naive Ideas Related to Sunrise, Sunset, Moonrise, and Moonset
- The sun actually rises in the east and sets in the west.
- The moon actually rises in the east and sets in the west.

Naive Ideas Related to Seasonal Change
- Some people think that the reason for the seasons on the earth is because the earth is farther away from the sun in the winter time.
- Some people think that the sun is "off-center" within our orbit, causing the earth to be closer to the sun at times during the year and farther away at other times.
- Some people are aware that the earth is tilted on its axis and think that the earth is closer to the sun at certain times of the year because of the tilt.

Naive Ideas Related to the Moon
- The moon shows one side toward the earth because it does not rotate.
- Some people think that when they see the moon during the day, it is not really the moon.
- The phases of the moon are caused by the shadow of the earth on the moon.
- The moon causes one tide per day.
- The moon has a dark side and a light side.

Solar System Concepts and Facts

The Moon: Earth's Satellite
- The moon is Earth's natural satellite.
- The moon orbits the earth about once a month, or every 27.3 days.
- The moon is 239,000 miles (384,000 km) from the earth.
- The moon's diameter is 2,160 miles (3,476 km).
- The moon's gravity is one-sixth that of Earth.
- The moon's gravity causes tides in the earth's oceans.
- The moon goes through daily changes, or phases, as it orbits the earth.
- The moon's phases are a result of the moon being round, the angle that it makes with the earth, and the sun's changes during its orbit.
- The moon appears to travel from east to west across the southern sky at night.
- The same side of the moon is always toward the earth because the moon rotates at the same rate that it revolves around the earth.
- The moon has a near side and a far side relative to the earth. We cannot see the far side from the earth's vantage point.
- All sides of the moon are illuminated as it orbits the earth. When the moon is in its new moon phase, the far side of the moon is illuminated. Hence, the moon does not have a permanent dark side and a permanent light side.
- A winter full moon is higher in the sky than a summer full moon.
- A new moon can eclipse the sun, and its shadow covers a small portion of the earth.
- A full moon can be eclipsed by the earth. This happens once or twice a year.

SOLAR SYSTEM CONCEPTS AND FACTS (CONT.)

A satellite is a small body that orbits around a larger body. The earth has one natural satellite, the moon. The moon orbits the earth once every 27.3 days. The moon orbits the earth nearly thirteen times each year. It is our closest neighbor at 239,000 miles (384,000 km). The moon's diameter is 2,160 miles (3,476 km) compared to the earth's diameter of 7,926 miles (12,756 km). The moon is one of the largest satellites in the solar system.

The moon's mass is a little over one/one-hundredth (0.0124) that of Earth's, and its gravitational pull is one-sixth the pull of gravity on Earth. As a result, there is no air on the moon. However, the moon's gravity causes tides on the earth; it causes the water in the oceans to rise and fall twice daily.

As the moon circles the earth, it goes through several phases. As it goes through its phases, it appears to change shape and is visible in different parts of the sky. The table below presents approximate times of the day for moonrise, the moon at its highest point in the sky, and moonset for each of several phases. The moon rotates once for every revolution of the earth; hence, the same side of the moon is always facing the earth.

About once or twice a year, the moon passes in the shadow of the earth during its full moon phase. This is called a lunar eclipse. More rarely, during the new moon phase, the moon's shadow blocks the sunlight from reaching the earth. This is called a solar eclipse. Because the moon's shadow is smaller than the earth's, a solar eclipse is visible only on a small portion of the earth.

	Symbol	Moonrise*	Highest Point*	Moonset*
New Moon		6 A.M.	12 noon	6 P.M.
Waxing Crescent		9 A.M.	3 P.M.	9 P.M.
First Quarter		12 noon	6 P.M.	12 midnight
Waxing Gibbous		3 P.M.	9 P.M.	3 A.M.
Full Moon		6 P.M.	12 midnight	6 A.M.
Waning Gibbous		9 P.M.	3 A.M.	9 A.M.
Third Quarter		12 midnight	6 A.M.	12 noon
Waning Crescent		3 A.M.	9 A.M.	3 P.M.
New Moon		6 A.M.	12 noon	6 P.M.

* *Note:* These times vary greatly, and this represents an approximation based on the position of the moon relative to the sun and the earth. More precise times are usually printed in the local newspaper and in a Farmer's Almanac.

SOLAR SYSTEM CONCEPTS AND FACTS (CONT.)

Measuring Time

- Time can be measured by observing the natural cycles of the sun and moon.
- Shadows cast by the sun can be used to measure and predict the passage of time during the day.
- The phases of the moon follow a cycle that can be used to measure and predict the passage of time during a month.
- The earth is spherical.
- The earth rotates once daily. This defines the day.
- The earth revolves about the sun once annually. This defines the year.
- The moon revolves around the earth about once a month.
- The earth is divided into 24 equally spaced meridians or longitude lines that are 15 degrees apart at the equator. These divisions define theoretical time zones.
- The earth is 24,888 miles (40,052 km) in circumference at the equator. Each time zone is about 1,000 miles (1,609 km) wide.
- In the Northern Hemisphere, the sun appears to travel across the southern sky from east to west during the day.
- The apparent motion of the sun across the sky is due to the earth rotating from west to east.
- Revolution refers to the orbit of a planet around the sun or a satellite around a planet.
- Rotation refers to the spin of a body in the solar system on its axis. The sun, Earth, moon, and the other planets all rotate.
- The sun's apparent motion: the sun appears to rise in the east and set in the west. In reality, it is the earth rotating from west to east; hence, we refer to the sun's apparent motion across the sky from east to west.

Seasonal Change on Earth

- The earth's orbit around the sun is elliptical; however, the orbit is nearly circular. Therefore, the earth's orbit is not the reason for seasonal change on the earth. It is, in fact, closer to the sun in January.
- The earth is tilted 23.5 degrees on its axis, and this tilt does not make a significant difference in the distance of the earth from the sun.
- The tilt of the earth remains constant as it orbits the sun. Therefore, the North Pole appears to point in the direction of the sun during June and away from the sun in December (Northern Hemisphere). Note that the opposite is true for the Southern Hemisphere. Since the South Pole points in the direction of the sun in December, summer begins there in December.
- The tilt of the earth is the reason for the variance observed in the length of the day during the year and therefore, the seasonal change on the earth.
- Latitude is the measure of angular distance north and south of the equator. Hence, any region of the earth may be noted relative to its distance from the equator by noting its latitude.
- Latitude is important relative to the amount of direct sunlight a region receives.

SOLAR SYSTEM CONCEPTS AND FACTS (CONT.)

- The Tropic of Cancer is an imaginary line (23.5 degrees north of the equator) representing the latitude farthest north at which the sun can shine directly overhead. The sun is directly overhead at noon at the Tropic of Cancer on the first day of summer in the Northern Hemisphere, around June 21.
- The Tropic of Capricorn is an imaginary line (23.5 degrees south of the equator) representing the farthest south at which the sun can shine directly overhead. The sun is directly overhead at noon at the Tropic of Capricorn on the first day of summer in the Southern Hemisphere, around December 21.
- The equator is an imaginary line, or great circle, equidistant from the Poles of the earth. The equator divides the earth into Northern and Southern Hemispheres. The equator represents zero degrees latitude. The sun is directly overhead at noon at the equator around March 21 and September 21. These dates are known as the equinoxes and represent the first day of spring and fall.
- The Arctic and Antarctic Circles represent imaginary lines circling the globe 23.5 degrees from the North and South Poles and represent the areas receiving 24 hours of daylight on June 21 for the Arctic Circle and December 21 for the Antarctic Circle.
- The horizon is the apparent intersection of the earth and the sky as seen by an observer on the earth.

Facts About the Planets

MERCURY

First planet in the solar system
Special Fact: Mercury rotates very slowly. It takes 59 Earth-days to rotate once.
Diameter: 3,031 miles (4,878 km)
Average distance from the sun: 36 million miles (58 million km)
Rotation: 58.7 Earth-days
Orbit of the sun: 88 Earth-days
Moons: None

VENUS

Second planet in the solar system
Special Fact: Venus has a thick atmosphere with crushing pressure. The clouds are made up of tiny droplets of acid.
Diameter: 7,521 miles (12,104 km)
Average distance from the sun: 67,200,000 miles (108,200,000 km)
Rotation: 243 Earth-days
Orbit of the sun: 224.7 Earth-days
Moons: None

SOLAR SYSTEM CONCEPTS AND FACTS (CONT.)

EARTH
Third planet in the solar system
Special Fact: Earth is one of the four small rocky planets that makes up the inner belt of planets. Earth is tilted on its axis 23.5 degrees and therefore has seasons.
Diameter: 7,926 miles (12,756 km)
Average distance from the sun: 93 million miles (150 million km)
Rotation: 23 hours, 56 minutes
Orbit of the sun: 365.25 days
Moons: 1

MARS
Fourth planet in the solar system
Special Fact: Mars is tilted on its axis 24 degrees, similar to Earth, and therefore, has seasons.
Diameter: 4,220 miles (6,794 km)
Average distance from the sun: 142 million miles (228 million km)
Rotation: 24 hours, 37 minutes
Orbit of the sun: 687 days
Moons: 2 (Phobos and Deimos)

Between the orbits of Mars and Jupiter is a wide belt of **asteroids**, or **planetoids**, that orbits the sun. Thousands of asteroids have been identified in this region of space. There are 26 asteroids that have a diameter of 125 miles (200 km) or larger. The largest three are Ceres, Pallas, and Vesta. Ceres has a diameter of 600 miles (950 km), Pallas and Vesta have diameters of 340 miles (550 km).

JUPITER
Fifth planet in the solar system
Special Fact: Jupiter is the largest planet. It is large enough to contain 1,000 bodies the size of Earth.
Diameter: 88,400 miles (142,000 km)
Average distance from the sun: 484 million miles (630 million km)
Jupiter rotates faster than any other planet; it takes less than 10 hours (9 hours, 50 minutes) for it to rotate.
Orbit of the sun: 11.9 years
Moons: 16 known
Four of Jupiter's largest moons can be observed with binoculars. They are referred to as the Galilean moons and include Io, Europa, Ganymede, and Callisto.

SOLAR SYSTEM CONCEPTS AND FACTS (CONT.)

Comets are a combination of ice, dust, and rock material and move in very eccentric orbits in some cases, carrying them beyond the orbits of all of the planets. Their orbits periodically carry some of them within the orbiting planets. They are characterized by a distinctive shape as they pass near the sun in their orbits. The shape includes a head and long, flowing, vapor tail.

SATURN
Sixth planet in the solar system
Special Fact: Saturn's interior includes a liquid metal layer that creates a strong magnetic field. The earth similarly has a magnetic field caused by an interior molten layer of metal. Saturn is known as the ringed planet. Scientists now know that Jupiter, Uranus, and Neptune also have rings.
Diameter: 74,600 miles (120,000 km)
Average distance from the sun: 887 million miles (1,430,000,000 km)
Rotation: 10 hours, 39 minutes
Orbit of the sun: 29.5 Earth-years
Moons: 18 known

URANUS
Seventh planet in the solar system
Special Fact: Uranus is the third-largest planet in the solar system. Uranus rotates on an axis that is almost tilted on its side. Sometimes its poles point directly at the sun.
Diameter: 31,700 miles (51,100 km)
Average distance from the sun: 1,784,000,000 miles (2,871,000,000 km)
Rotation: 17 hours, 14 minutes
Orbit of the sun: 84 years
Moons: 17 known

SOLAR SYSTEM CONCEPTS AND FACTS (CONT.)

NEPTUNE

Eighth planet in the solar system
Special Fact: Neptune rotates on a nearly upright axis.
Diameter: 30,800 miles (49,500 km)
Average distance from the sun: 2,794,000,000 miles (4,498,000,000 km)
Rotation: 16 hours, 7 minutes
Orbit of the sun: 163.7 years
Moons: 8 known

PLUTO

Ninth planet in the solar system
Special Fact: Many astronomers question whether Pluto should be classified as a planet. It is the outermost planet most of the time; however, its eccentric orbit carries it inside the orbit of Neptune occasionally.
Diameter: 1,484 miles (2,390 km)
Average distance from the sun: 3,700,000,000 miles (5,900,000,000 km)
Rotation: 6 days, 9 hours, 36 minutes
Orbit of the sun: 248 years
Moons: 1 known

NATIONAL STANDARDS

NSES Content Standards (NRC, 1996)
National Research Council (1996). *National Science Education Standards.* Washington,
    D.C.: National Academy Press.

Unifying Concepts: K–12
Systems, Order, and Organization

The natural and designed world is complex. Scientists and students learn to define small portions for the convenience of investigation. The units of investigation can be referred to as systems. A system is an organized group of related objects or components that form a whole. Systems can consist of electrical circuits, living systems, the solar system, etc. Order implies that the behavior of units of matter, objects, organisms, or events can be described statistically. Organization includes models, tables, etc., that are used to present, describe, and organize information.

Systems, Order, and Organization

The goal of this standard is to ...
- Think and analyze in terms of systems.
- Assume that the behavior of the universe is not capricious. Nature is predictable.
- Understand the regularities in a system.
- Understand that prediction is the use of knowledge to identify and explain observations.
- Understand that the behavior of matter, objects, organisms, or events has order and can be described statistically.

Evidence, Models, and Explanation

The goal of this standard is to ...
- Recognize that evidence consists of observations and data on which to base scientific explanations.
- Recognize that models have explanatory power.
- Recognize that scientific explanations incorporate existing scientific knowledge (laws, principles, theories, paradigms, models) and new evidence from observations, experiments, or models.
- Recognize that scientific explanations should reflect a rich scientific knowledge base, evidence of logic, higher levels of analysis, greater tolerance of criticism and uncertainty, and a clear demonstration of the relationship between logic, evidence, and current knowledge.

Change, Constancy, and Measurement

The goal of this standard is to …
- Recognize that some properties of objects are characterized by constancy, including the speed of light, the charge of an electron, and the total mass plus energy of the universe.
- Recognize that changes might occur in the properties of materials, position of objects, motion, and form and function of systems.
- Recognize that changes in systems can be quantified.
- Recognize that measurement systems may be used to clarify observations.

NATIONAL STANDARDS (CONT.)

Form and Function
The goal of this standard is to …
- Recognize that the form of an object is frequently related to its use, operation, or function.
- Recognize that function frequently relies on form.
- Recognize that form and function apply to different levels of organization.
- Be able to explain function by referring to form and explain form by referring to function.

NSES Content Standard A: Inquiry
- Abilities necessary to do scientific inquiry are to ...
  - Identify questions that can be answered through scientific investigations.
  - Design and conduct a scientific investigation.
  - Use appropriate tools and techniques to gather, analyze, and interpret data.
  - Develop descriptions, explanations, predictions, and models using evidence.
  - Think critically and logically to make relationships between evidence and explanations.
  - Recognize and analyze alternative explanations and predictions.
  - Communicate scientific procedures and explanations.
  - Use mathematics in all aspects of scientific inquiry.

- Understanding about inquiry means that ...
  - Different kinds of questions suggest different kinds of scientific investigations.
  - Current scientific knowledge and understanding guide scientific investigations.
  - Mathematics is important in all aspects of scientific inquiry.
  - Technology used to gather data enhances accuracy and allows scientists to analyze and quantify results of investigations.
  - Scientific explanations emphasize evidence, have logically consistent arguments, and use scientific principles, models, and theories.
  - Science advances through legitimate skepticism.
  - Scientific investigations sometimes result in new ideas and phenomena for study, generate new methods or procedures, or develop new technologies to improve data collection.

NSES Content Standard D: Earth and Space Science
- Earth in the Solar System
  - Earth is the third planet from the sun in a system that includes the moon, the sun, eight other planets and their moons, and smaller objects, such as asteroids and comets. The sun, an average star, is the central and largest body in the solar system.
  - Describe the organization and physical characteristics of the solar system (e.g., sun, planets, satellites, asteroids, and comets). This is an example of a benchmark from the Illinois Learning Standards, Illinois State Board of Education, Springfield, Illinois.
  - Most objects in the solar system are in regular and predictable motion. Those motions explain such phenomena as the day, the year, phases of the moon, and eclipses.
  - Gravity is the force that keeps planets in orbit around the sun and governs the rest of the motion in the solar system. Gravity alone holds us to the earth's surface and explains the phenomena of tides.

NATIONAL STANDARDS (CONT.)

- Simulate, analyze, and explain the effects of gravitational force in the solar system (e.g., orbital shape and speed, tides, spherical shape of the planets and the moon). This is an example of a benchmark from the Illinois Learning Standards, Illinois State Board of Education, Springfield, Illinois.
- The sun is the major source of energy for phenomena on the earth's surface, such as the growth of plants, winds, ocean currents, and the water cycle. Seasons result from variations in the amount of sun's energy hitting the surface, due to the tilt of the earth's axis and the length of the day.

NSES Content Standard F: Science in Personal and Social Perspectives 5–8
- Science and technology in society means that ...
  - Science influences society through its knowledge and world view.
  - Societal challenges often inspire questions for scientific research.
  - Technology influences society through its products and processes.
  - Scientists and engineers work in many different settings.
  - Science cannot answer all questions, and technology cannot solve all human problems.

NSES Content Standard G: History and Nature of Science 5–8
- Science as a human endeavor
  - Women and men of various social and ethnic backgrounds—and with diverse interests, talents, qualities, and motivations—engage in the activities of science, engineering, and related fields such as the health professions. Some scientists work in teams, and some work alone, but all communicate extensively with others.
  - Science requires different abilities, depending on such factors as study and type of inquiry. Science is very much a human endeavor, and the work of science relies on basic human qualities, such as reasoning, insight, energy, skill, and creativity, as well as habits of mind, such as intellectual honesty, tolerance of ambiguity, skepticism, and openness to new ideas.
- Nature of science
  - Scientists formulate and test their explanations of nature using observation, experiments, and theoretical and mathematical models.
  - It is normal for scientists to differ with one another about interpretation of evidence and theory.
  - It is part of scientific inquiry for scientists to evaluate the results of other scientists' work.
- History of Science
  - Many individuals have contributed to the traditions of science.
  - Science has been and is practiced by different individuals in different cultures.
  - Tracing the history of science can show how difficult it was for scientific innovators to break through the accepted ideas of their time to reach the conclusions we now accept.

NATIONAL STANDARDS (CONT.)

> **Principles and Standards for School Mathematics (NCTM, 2000)**
> National Council of Teachers of Mathematics. (2000). *Principles and Standards for School Mathematics.* Reston, VA: National Council of Teachers of Mathematics.

Number and Operations
Students will be enabled to ...
- Understand numbers, ways of representing numbers, relationships among numbers, and number systems.
- Understand meanings of operations and how they relate to one another.
- Compute fluently and make reasonable estimates.

Algebra
Students will be enabled to ...
- Understand patterns, relations, and functions.
- Represent and analyze mathematical situations and structures using algebraic symbols.
- Use mathematical models to represent and understand quantitative relationships.
- Analyze change in various contexts.

Geometry
Students will be enabled to ...
- Analyze characteristics and properties of two- and three-dimensional geometric shapes and develop mathematical arguments about geometric relationships.
- Specify locations and describe spatial relationships using coordinate geometry and other representational systems.
- Apply transformations and use symmetry to analyze mathematical situations.
- Use visualization, spatial reasoning, and geometric modeling to solve problems.

Measurement
Students will be enabled to ...
- Understand measurable attributes of objects and the units, systems, and processes of measurement.
- Apply appropriate techniques, tools, and formulas to determine measurements.

Data Analysis and Probability
Students will be enabled to ...
- Formulate questions that can be addressed with data and collect, organize, and display relevant data to answer them.
- Select and use appropriate statistical methods to analyze data.
- Develop and evaluate inferences and predictions that are based on data.
- Understand and apply basic concepts of probability.

SCIENCE PROCESS SKILLS

Introduction:
Science is organized curiosity, and an important part of this organization is the thinking skills or information-processing skills. We ask the question "Why?" and then must plan a strategy for answering the question or questions. In the process of answering our questions, we make and carefully record observations, make predictions, identify and control variables, measure, make inferences, and communicate our findings. Additional skills may be called upon depending on the nature of our questions. In this way, science is a verb involving active manipulation of materials and careful thinking. Science is dependent on language, math, and reading skills as well as the specialized thinking skills associated with identifying and solving problems.

BASIC PROCESS SKILLS

Classifying: Grouping, ordering, arranging or distributing objects, events, or information into categories based on properties or criteria, according to some method or system.

> **Example** – The skill is being demonstrated if the student is …
> Using the attributes of the planets in our solar system to complete a sort of the planets. Attributes might include planet size, length of day, length of year, and number of moons.

Observing: Using the senses (or extensions of the senses) to gather information about an object or event.

> **Example** – The skill is being demonstrated if the student is …
> Conducting a study of the phases of the moon over a period of a month. This would include daily observations and the relative shape of the moon, position in the sky, and the times that it rises and sets.

Measuring: Using both standard and nonstandard measures or estimates to describe the dimensions of an object or event. Making quantitative observations.

> **Example** – The skill is being demonstrated if the student …
> Sets up a shadow stick and records the shadows cast by the sun for a given period of time, such as a day. The shadows can then be measured for relative length and orientation to compass direction.

Inferring: Making an interpretation or conclusion based on reasoning to explain an observation.

> **Example** – The skill is being demonstrated if the student is…
> Interpreting information from a set of observations and measurements of a shadow stick. Inferences might include what the shadow might look like at different times of the month or year.

SCIENCE PROCESS SKILLS (CONT.)

Communicating: Ideas through speaking or writing. Students may share the results of investigations, collaborate on solving problems and gather and interpret data both orally and in writing, using graphs, charts, and diagrams to describe data.

> **Example** – The skill is being demonstrated if the student is ...
> Describing an event or a set of observations (phases of the moon); participating in brainstorming and hypothesizing before an investigation; formulating initial and follow-up questions in the study of a topic; summarizing data, interpreting findings, and offering conclusions; questioning or refuting previous findings; making decisions; using a graph to show the length of daylight hours over the period of a year.

Predicting: Making a forecast of future events or conditions in the context of previous observations and experiences.

> **Example** – The skill is being demonstrated if the student is ...
> Predicting the phases of the moon for a month following a set of observations or predicting the length of a solar shadow for a time period other than one for which observations were made.

Manipulating Materials: Handling or treating materials and equipment skillfully and effectively.

> **Example** – The skill is being demonstrated if the student is ...
> Using astronomy instruments for measuring the angle of the moon or sun above the horizon. Such instruments might include an astrolabe or clinometer.

Replicating: Performing acts that duplicate demonstrated symbols, patterns, or procedures.

> **Example** – The skill is being demonstrated if the student is ...
> Making observations on the positions of the observable moons of Jupiter over a period of ten days to two weeks to replicate the observations that Galileo made in 1609.

Using Numbers: Applying mathematical rules or formulas to calculate quantities or determine relationships from basic measurements.

> **Example** – The skill is being demonstrated if the student is...
> Comparing the relative distances of the planets from the sun; comparing the periods of revolution about the sun for each planet; using the two sets of data to establish a correlation.

SCIENCE PROCESS SKILLS (CONT.)

Developing Vocabulary: Specialized terminology and unique uses of common words in relation to a given topic need to be identified and given meaning.

> **Example** – The skill is being demonstrated if the student is …
> Using context clues, working definitions, glossaries or dictionaries, word structure (roots, prefixes, suffixes), and synonyms and antonyms to clarify meaning; researching the historical origin for the names of the planets, their moons, and other celestial objects in our solar system.

Questioning: Questions serve to focus inquiry, determine prior knowledge, and establish purposes or expectations for an investigation. An active search for information is promoted when questions are used. Questioning may also be used in the context of assessing student learning.

> **Example** – The skill is being demonstrated if the student is …
> Using what is already known about a topic or concept to formulate questions for further investigation; hypothesizing and predicting prior to gathering data; or formulating questions as new information is acquired. Such broad questions as the following can lead to developing concepts about the observable cycles in the solar system: Where is the moon? Where was the moon? How do the daylight hours change over the year? What is the reason for the seasons? How is time measured?

Using Cues: Key words and symbols convey significant meaning in messages. Organizational patterns facilitate comprehension of major ideas. Graphic features clarify textual information.

> **Example** – The skill is being demonstrated if the student is …
> Listing or underlining words and phrases that carry the most important details, or relating key words together to express a main idea or concept.

INTEGRATED PROCESS SKILLS

Creating Models: Displaying information by means of graphic illustrations or other multisensory representations.

> **Example** – The skill is being demonstrated if the student is …
> Drawing a graph or diagram; constructing a three-dimensional object; using a digital camera to record an event; constructing a chart or table; or producing a picture or diagram that illustrates the phases of the moon. Students may also make models of the solar system to illustrate the relative position and size of the planets.

SCIENCE PROCESS SKILLS (CONT.)

Formulating Hypotheses: Stating or constructing a statement that is testable about what is thought to be the expected outcome of an experiment (based on reasoning).

> **Example** – The skill is being demonstrated if the student is …
> Making a statement to be used as the basis for a set of observations or experiment: "The relative position of the earth in its orbit, combined with the angle of tilt in the earth's axis is responsible for seasonal change on the earth. If the tilt of the axis were to change, then the seasons would also be affected." Students could use light sources and a globe to investigate the effects of these changes.

Generalizing: Drawing general conclusions from particulars.

> **Example** – The skill is being demonstrated if the student is …
> Making a summary statement following analysis of experimental results: "Seasonal change on the earth is related to the position of the earth in its orbit and the tilt of the earth on its axis."

Identifying and Controlling Variables: Recognizing the characteristics of objects or factors in events that are constant or change under different conditions and that can affect an experimental outcome, keeping most variables constant while manipulating only one variable.

> **Example** – The skill is being demonstrated if the student is …
> Listing or describing the factors that are thought to influence the length of a solar shadow and its alignment to a compass direction at any given time.

Defining Operationally: Stating how to measure a variable in an experiment and defining a variable according to the actions or operations to be performed on or with it.

> **Example** – The skill is being demonstrated if the student is …
> Defining such things as the time of day in the context of the materials and actions for a specific activity. Hence, the time of day might be described relative to a shadow stick and the compass direction that is observed for a shadow, as well as the relative length of the shadow.

Recording and Interpreting Data: Collecting bits of information about objects and events that illustrate a specific situation; organizing and analyzing data that have been obtained; and drawing conclusions from it by determining apparent patterns or relationships in the data.

> **Example** – The skill is being demonstrated if the student is …
> Recording data (taking notes, making lists/outlines, recording numbers on charts/graphs, making tape recordings, taking photographs, writing numbers of results of observations/ measurements) from the series of observations made of the moon, its position in the sky relative to time of day, and the phase of the moon observed and recorded.

21

SCIENCE PROCESS SKILLS (CONT.)

Making Decisions: Identifying alternatives and choosing a course of action from among alternatives after basing the judgment for the selection on justifiable reasons.

> **Example** – The skill is being demonstrated if the student is ...
> Identifying alternative ways to measure time and design devices such as sundials to observe and record time accurately.

Experimenting: Being able to conduct an experiment, including asking an appropriate question, stating a hypothesis, identifying and controlling variables, operationally defining those variables, designing a "fair" experiment, and interpreting the results of an experiment.

> **Example** – The skill is being demonstrated if the student is ...
> Utilizing the entire process of designing, building, and testing various devices to measure time; arranging equipment and materials to conduct an investigation; manipulating the equipment and materials; and conducting the investigation.

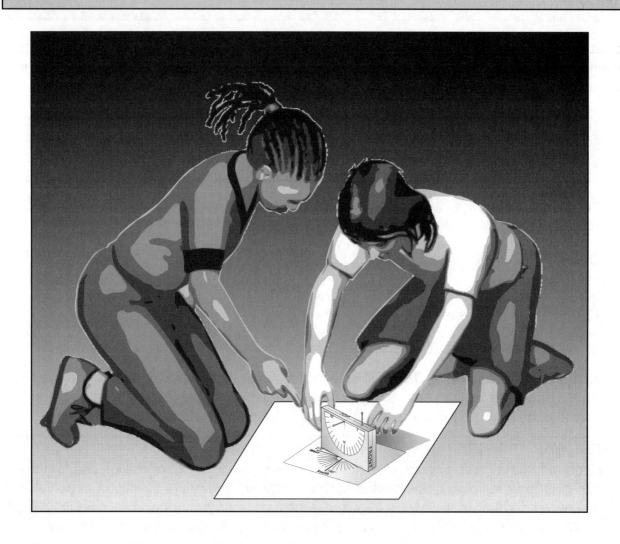

STUDENT INQUIRY ACTIVITY **1**: TIME AND THE SHADOW STICK

Topic: Daytime astronomy: Observations on the change in shadows cast by the sun.

Science and Mathematics Standards:

NSES: Unifying Concepts and Processes including Systems, Order, and Organization; Evidence, Models, and Explanation; and Constancy, Change, and Measurement; Content Standard A: Inquiry; Content Standard D: Earth and Space Science; and Content Standard G: History and Nature of Science

NCTM: Geometry, Measurement, and Data Analysis and Probability

See **National Standards section** for more details.

Science Concepts:
- The apparent motion of the sun causes shadows to change throughout the day.
- Time can be predicted and measured using a shadow stick.
- Shadow sticks can be used to determine compass direction.
- The shortest shadow of the day is at midday or solar noon.
- Solar noon is represented by the shortest shadow for any given day.*
- Solar noon may also be called midday. Midday is the halfway point between sunrise and sunset.**
- True north may be found by observing and recording the shadow at solar noon.

*   A farmer's almanac can be used to approximate solar noon for your area. Sun time is not standard time or daylight saving time. *Example:* Solar noon on March 21, 2003, in Boston, Massachusetts, was 11:52 A.M. and in Indianapolis, Indiana, was 12:48 P.M. This is because Indianapolis is on the western edge of the eastern time zone. This also explains why Indianapolis doesn't observe daylight saving time in the summer.

**   The local newspaper may include the time for sunrise and sunset for your city. This information could be used to verify your observations and predict when the shadow will be at its shortest (midday).

See **Naive Ideas and Solar System Concepts and Facts section** for more details.

Science Skills:
        You will make **observations** of shadows cast by the sun at various times during the day, week, month, and year. You will make **inferences** about the apparent motion of the sun and the earth and about how the shadows that you observe may be used to **predict** and **measure** time. You will **collect data**, including information about the length of shadows and the direction in which the shadows point at various times of the day.

See **Science Process Skills section** for descriptions and examples.

23

Student Inquiry Activity 1: Time and the Shadow Stick (cont.)

Materials:
Per group: one 2–3 inch long piece of 1/2-inch diameter dowel
11″ x 16″ piece of cardboard
Piece of clay to support the dowel
Sidewalk chalk
2 pieces of 8.5″ x 11″ copy paper

Content Background:
Sundials have been used for centuries to measure time by following the regular pattern of shadows cast by the sun's apparent motion across the sky. Actually, the earth rotates from west to east; therefore, shadows move from west to east. From locations in the northern half of the earth, or the Northern Hemisphere, shadows point to the west in the morning, point north at noon, and point to the east in the afternoon.

In this activity, the dowel will be used to cast a shadow on the base made up of a piece of cardboard covered with copy paper. The shadow stick (dowel) and cardboard base are placed in a sunny spot on a sidewalk, and students trace the shadow cast by the dowel on the paper at different times during the day. It is important to position the shadow stick in the center of the cardboard for this activity.

This activity is intended to introduce general concepts about shadows for the Northern Hemisphere. A shadow stick will cast a shadow that moves in an arc from the west, and through the north to the east, as the day progresses from sunrise to sunset. Shadows are longest at sunrise and sunset and shortest at midday or solar noon. The solar noon shadow points directly north. Solar noon is defined as the time when the sun is highest in the sky for any given day and may not coincide with noon on your watch.

Challenge Question: How does a shadow change during the day?

Procedure:
1. Prior to going outside, have the students predict the direction of orientation for the shadow relative to the school building and other landmarks.
2. Place a vertical dowel in the center of the cardboard base covered with copy paper, using a piece of clay to support the dowel upright. Place the cardboard base and shadow stick on a relatively level place and observe its shadow.
3. Use a piece of chalk to outline the base of the rectangular piece of cardboard on the sidewalk where it rests. Outline the piece of clay supporting the wooden dowel with a pencil.
4. You may also make observations of permanent shadow sticks such as fence posts or flagpoles.
5. Make a record by tracing the shadow on the blank piece of paper that you have placed on top of the cardboard base. Record the time that you made your first shadow outline on that outline.
6. Leave the setup on the sidewalk, and trace the shadows made on the paper at regular intervals.

Name: _____ Date:_____

STUDENT INQUIRY ACTIVITY 1: TIME AND THE SHADOW STICK (CONT.)

You will need to set up a shadow stick like the one in the diagram below.

Materials:
Dowel
Cardboard Base
Clay
Chalk

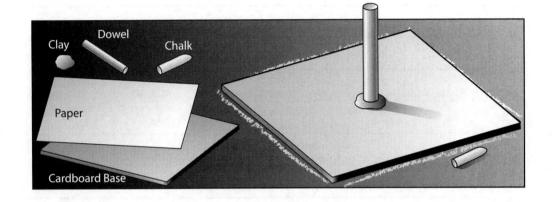

Exploration/Data Collection:

A. Predict: In what direction will the shadow be pointing?

_____

B. Predict: How long will the shadow be?

_____

C. Measure: In what direction is the shadow pointing?

_____

D. Measure: How long is the shadow?

_____

E. Will the shadow change in half an hour? How?

_____

F. Will the shadow change in one hour? How?

_____

G. Where is the shadow relative to the direction of the sun?

_____

H. Where is the sun in the morning?

_____

Name: _____ Date:_____

STUDENT INQUIRY ACTIVITY 1: TIME AND THE SHADOW STICK (CONT.)

I. Where is the shadow in the afternoon?

_____

J. When is the shadow longest?

_____

K. When is the shadow shortest?

_____

L. Where is the sun at noon?

_____

M. Is there a shadow at noon?

_____

Conclusions:

A. What can we learn by watching shadows?

_____

_____

_____

_____

B. What causes the shadow to move or change during the day?

_____

_____

_____

C. What are the general patterns in the shadow's position relative to the time of the day observed?

_____

_____

_____

_____

Name: _____ Date:_____

STUDENT INQUIRY ACTIVITY **1**: TIME AND THE SHADOW STICK (CONT.)

Assessment: Check each item if it is completed correctly.

A. The Shadow Stick
_____ The shadow stick is set up correctly.

B. Exploration/Data Collection (Northern Hemisphere)
_____ C: The shadow will point roughly west in the morning, north around noon, and east in the afternoon.

_____ D: The length of the shadow will vary depending on the length of the shadow stick and the time of day. Generally, shadows are longest in the early morning after sunrise and in the afternoon just before sunset and the shortest at midday.

_____ E: Yes, the shadow will move in an arc from the west through the north to the east as the day progresses.

_____ F: Yes, the shadow will move in an arc from the west through the north to the east as the day progresses. Note the difference in the amount of movement for an hour compared to a half-hour.

_____ G: The shadow is in the opposite direction of the sun.

_____ H: The sun is generally in the east in the morning

_____ I: The shadow is generally in the east in the afternoon.

_____ J: The shadow is longest at sunrise and sunset.

_____ K: The shadow is shortest at solar noon or when the sun is highest in the sky.

_____ L: The sun is in the south at noon.

_____ M: Yes, for areas in the United States or for any area in the Northern Hemisphere above the Tropic of Cancer (23.5 degrees latitude).

C. Conclusions
_____ A: We learn that the shadow is constantly changing during the daylight hours and that it moves in an arc from the west through the north to the east as the day progresses from sunrise to sunset. We can begin to approximate the time of day by observing the shadow's location. The length of the shadow is longest at sunrise and sunset and shortest at noon.

_____ B: We observe the sun moving across the sky and infer that it is the rotation of the earth and apparent motion of the sun that causes the shadows to change during the day.

_____ C: The pattern observed includes the change in shadow length. Shadows grow shorter from sunrise to noon and longer from noon to sunset. The second major pattern is that the shadow moves from the west through the north to the east as daylight progresses from sunrise to sunset.

STUDENT INQUIRY ACTIVITY 2 : OBSERVING A TIME ZONE PASS

Topic: Daytime Astronomy: Time Zones

National Standards, Science Concepts, Science Skills: (See Student Inquiry Activity 1.)

Introduction:

In this activity as in the last, we will be observing the change in shadows as the day progresses. This time, however, we will be paying closer attention to two factors. By aligning the shadow stick and board with the north, we will be able to track and observe the compass direction in which the shadows point at various times during the day. Secondly, by making our observations exactly one hour apart, we can measure the number of degrees the shadow changes each hour.

You will need to set up a shadow stick like the one in the diagram below.

Materials:
Copy paper
Cardboard base
Plastic straw or stirrer
Plaster of Paris
Chalk
Magnetic compass
Protractor

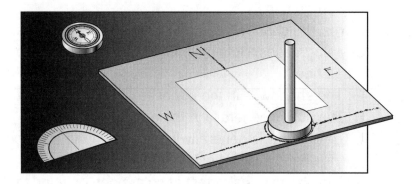

Procedure:
1. For this activity, we suggest that you construct a shadow stick by embedding a plastic straw or stirrer in a base of plaster of Paris. Be sure to align your stirrer perpendicular to the base before you pour the plaster.
2. Draw a line perpendicular to the bottom edge of the cardboard base.
3. Place your shadow stick at the center of the south edge of a cardboard base covered with copy paper, and align the shadow stick with the line drawn on the cardboard base.
4. Use a magnetic compass to align the entire system north and south. Note: Magnetic north and true north are not usually the same for most areas in the Northern Hemisphere.
5. Be sure that the cardboard base and shadow stick are relatively level. We recommend taping or weighing the base down to avoid having it moved by the wind.
6. Use a piece of chalk to outline the base of the rectangular piece of cardboard on the sidewalk where it rests. Outline the base of the shadow stick with a pencil.
7. Make a record by tracing the shadow on the blank piece of paper that you have placed on top of the cardboard base. Record the time that you made your first shadow outline on that outline.
8. Leave the setup on the sidewalk and trace the shadows made on the paper precisely one hour later. Try to make at least two observations that are spaced precisely one hour apart.
9. Using a protractor, measure the angle made by the shadows that are spaced at one-hour intervals.

Name: _____ Date:_____

STUDENT INQUIRY ACTIVITY 2: OBSERVING A TIME ZONE PASS (CONT.)

Exploration/Data Collection:

A. Using a protractor, measure the angle made by two shadows that are precisely one hour apart. What angle is observed?

_____

B. What conclusion can be drawn from your finding?

_____

_____

C. What time of the day would you expect to observe shadows pointing in a westerly direction?

_____

D. What time of the day would you expect to observe shadows pointing in an easterly direction?

_____

E. What time of the day would you expect to observe shadows pointing in a northerly direction?

_____

F. Will the noon shadow change in one month? Three months? How?

_____

_____

_____

G. How does the shadow change as the year progresses?

_____

_____

_____

H. How can you tilt your shadow stick so the shadow disappears?

_____

_____

Name: _____ Date: _____

Summary:

What is being observed in this activity is the change in shadow direction and length due to the rotation of the earth and the apparent position of the sun in the sky because of the rotation. Generally speaking, in the Northern Hemisphere, the shadow points to the west in the morning as the sun rises in the east, points to the north at solar noon, and points to the east in the afternoon as the sun sets in the west. The apparent motion of the sun is explained by understanding that the earth rotates from west toward the east on a 24-hour, or daily, cycle. The shadow length in this activity can be described in the following way: the shadows at sunrise and sunset are the longest, and the shadow cast by the sun when it is at its highest point in the sky (solar noon) is the shortest.

Shadows also change as the earth travels around the sun (revolution). One revolution of the earth about the sun represents one year. If you observe the shadow at the same time each day over several weeks, you will notice changes as well.

For each hour of rotation, the earth passes through 15 degrees of rotation. This represents a time zone. If you divide 360 degrees by 15 degrees, you arrive at 24 equal periods.

Real-World Application:

As the earth makes its annual trek about the sun, we pass through the four seasons of the year. The angle of the sun in the sky at noon above the horizon changes dramatically. For instance, for Chicago's latitude, the sun is at 24.7 degrees above the horizon on December 21 (winter) and is at 71.6 degrees above the horizon on June 21 (summer). The length of daylight for Chicago is a little over 9 hours on December 21, about 12 hours on March 21 and September 21, and over 15 hours on June 21. Of course, the impact of this change in solar input affects the weather, growing season, and the clothing that we wear, among a whole array of other effects.

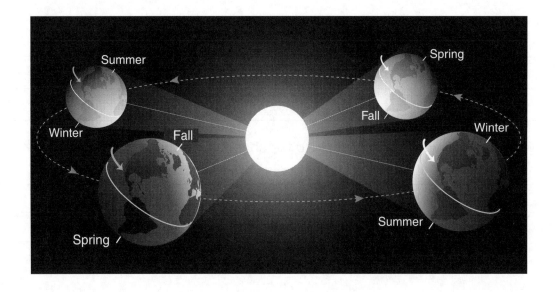

The Solar System   Student Inquiry Activity 2: Observing a Time Zone Pass

Name: _____ Date:_____

STUDENT INQUIRY ACTIVITY 2: OBSERVING A TIME ZONE PASS (CONT.)

Assessment: Answers to Exploration/Data Collection Questions

A. The angle observed should be within one degree of 15 degrees. Students who have accurately set up their shadow sticks and have made measurements precisely one hour apart should arrive at a 15-degree measurement. The earth rotates 15 degrees each hour. "You have just observed a time zone pass!"

B. The earth rotates at a constant rate, and this can be observed and measured. Note that the speed of rotation varies with latitude; however, the earth rotates over 1,000 miles per hour at the equator. We are spinning at the rate of 1,000 miles an hour!

C. Shadows are generally oriented in a westerly direction in the Northern Hemisphere during the morning hours.

D. Shadows are generally oriented in an easterly direction in the Northern Hemisphere during the afternoon hours.

E. Shadows are generally oriented in a northerly direction in the Northern Hemisphere around noon. Solar noon is defined as the time when a shadow is cast directly north.

F. Yes, the shadows are constantly changing since the earth's orbit, combined with the tilt of the earth at 23.5 degrees, causes the sun to appear at different heights in the sky. The orientation of the earth to the sun because of this tilt also means that the sun will rise and set at different times each day. Generally speaking, shadows grow longer as we approach winter and shorter as we approach summer. This is assuming that we are making observations at approximately the same time each day.

G. Shadows grow longer as we move from the summer solstice (June 21) to the winter solstice (December 21) and shorter as we move from the winter solstice to the summer solstice.

H. If we angle the shadow stick so that it is pointing directly at the sun, we can make its shadow all but disappear. The angle that the shadow stick makes with the ground when it is pointed directly at the sun represents an angle showing the sun's height in the sky.

STUDENT INQUIRY ACTIVITY 3 : SKY DOMES

Topic: Daytime astronomy: Modeling the sun's apparent path across the sky

---

Science and Mathematics Standards:

NSES: Unifying Concepts and Processes including Systems, Order, and Organization; Evidence, Models, and Explanation; and Constancy, Change, and Measurement. Content Standard A: Inquiry, Content Standard D: Earth and Space Science, and Content Standard G: History and Nature of Science

NCTM: Measurement and Data Analysis and Probability

See **National Standards section** for additional information.

Science Concepts:
- In the Northern Hemisphere of Earth, the sun appears to cross the sky from east to west through the southern sky.
- The apparent motion of the sun can be modeled using a hemisphere-shaped dome or wire strainer to create a sky dome.
- A sky dome model can be used to model the position of the sun in the sky at any time during the daylight hours.
- The relative position of an observer on Earth and the rotation of the earth is responsible for the apparent movement of the sun from the east (sunrise) through the south (noon) to the west (sunset) in the Northern Hemisphere.

See **Naive Ideas and Solar System Concepts and Facts section** for more details.

Science Skills:
   You will use a large half-dome wire strainer to **model** the apparent path of the sun across the sky. **Observations** can be made at regular intervals during the daylight hours to note the apparent position of the sun in the sky. **Inferences** can be made about the actual rotation of the earth from west to east from the observations of the change in position of the sun during the day. You will **collect** and **analyze data** to determine the relative times and positions of the sun during the day. **Predictions** can be made for future dates concerning the relative position of the sun at various times during the day. **Measurements** can be made to determine the angle of the sun's height relative to the horizon at specified times during the day. A magnetic compass can be used to determine the relative direction of the sun at various times during the day.

See **Science Process Skills section** for descriptions and examples.

Content Background:
   One of the ways to record the sun's apparent path directly on a sunny day is with a large kitchen strainer and several beaded straight pins. You will need a strainer made with fine mesh that is shaped as nearly as possible like a half-globe.

32

STUDENT INQUIRY ACTIVITY 3 : SKY DOMES (CONT.)

As the earth rotates, the apparent motion of the sun across the sky for observers in the Northern Hemisphere is from southeast to southwest in an arc. In everyday language we say, "The sun rises in the east and sets in the west."

In this model, the strainer represents the sky from horizon to horizon in all directions. The base represents the earth, and the dot in the middle of the base represents you, the observer.

Materials (per group):
Large dome-shaped kitchen strainer
Beaded straight pins
Marking pen
Chalk
Either a white plastic container lid the size of the strainer or a rectangular piece of cardboard.
**A magnetic compass is an optional piece of equipment that would be useful in this activity.

Challenge Question: What is the (apparent) path of the sun across the sky?

Procedure:
1. Trace the outline of the strainer on a recording surface.
2. Trace the outline of the entire setup on the sidewalk with the chalk. It's important that the strainer remain oriented the same way for the period of the observations.
3. Find the center of the circle that the edge of the strainer makes on the recording surface.
4. Place a dot at the center of this circle. In this model, the dot becomes your observer, or represents you on the surface of the earth. The strainer represents a model of the sky overhead.
5. Hold the straight pin so that the shadow of the round head is cast onto the observer dot inside the strainer on the base or "surface of the earth."
6. Place the pin through the mesh in the strainer so that the shadow remains over the observer dot.
7. Repeat this with other pins several times during the day.
8. Starting in the morning and finishing in the late afternoon, place several pins in the strainer to represent and model the apparent path of the sun across the sky. Note that the resulting record that you have for the apparent path of the sun across the sky is for that date. That is the date that the observations were made. The path changes as we move through the year, or as the earth travels around the sun. To retain this record on the strainer, you might thread yarn through the strainer joining the points made by the heads of the pins.

Extensions:
Option 1: You may want to have students use a magnetic compass to record the position of the sun relative to time and compass direction.

Option 2: You may want to measure the angle of the sun's height above the horizon for specific times during the day. For instance: What is the height of the sun above the horizon for solar noon? *Note:* Solar noon may be defined as the time of day when the shadow cast by the sun is oriented directly north.

Name: _____ Date: _____

STUDENT INQUIRY ACTIVITY **3**: SKY DOMES (CONT.)

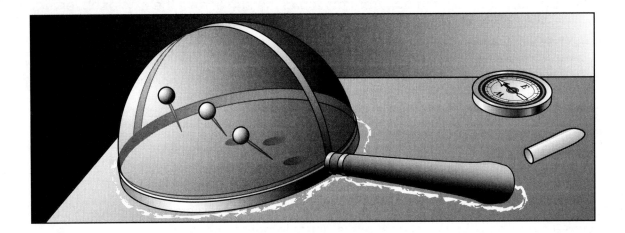

You will need to set up a "sky dome" like the one in the drawing above.

Materials:
Wire strainer
Beaded straight pins
Base (i.e., large plastic lid or rectangular piece of cardboard)
Chalk

Procedure:
1. Trace the outline of the strainer on a recording surface.
2. Trace the outline of the entire setup on the sidewalk with the chalk.
3. It's important that the strainer remains oriented the same way for the period of the observations.
4. The base should have a dot representing an observer on Earth at its center.
5. Hold the straight pin so that the shadow of the round head is cast onto the observer dot inside the strainer on the base or "surface of the earth."
6. Place the pin through the mesh in the strainer so that the shadow remains over the observer dot.
7. Repeat this with other pins several times during the day.
8. Starting in the morning and finishing in the late afternoon, place several pins in the strainer to represent and model the apparent path of the sun across the sky.

Exploration/Data Collection:

A. Predict: Where will the "modeled sun" (pinhead) be on the strainer for your first observation?

_____

B. Predict: Where will the "modeled sun" be one hour from now?

_____

Name: _____ Date:_____

STUDENT INQUIRY ACTIVITY 3: SKY DOMES (CONT.)

Make observations and place pins in the strainer throughout a school day, starting in the morning and completing the work at the end of the school day.

C. What is the time of day that a pin is at the highest point on the strainer?

_____

D. What is the time of day that a pin is at the lowest point on the strainer?

_____

E. What is the pattern of the path of the sun across the sky?

_____

F. Will the pattern be the same tomorrow?

_____

G. Will the pattern be the same in one month? Two months? Three months?

_____

_____

H. What would the path look like in the summer?

_____

I. What would the path look like in the winter?

_____

J. What would the path look like in the fall?

_____

K. What would the path look like in the spring?

_____

L. Is the sun ever directly overhead for the observer? Why or why not?

_____

_____

Name: _____ Date:_____

STUDENT INQUIRY ACTIVITY 3 : SKY DOMES (CONT.)

Conclusions:

A. What can we learn from observing the sun over a period of daylight?

_____

_____

_____

B. What is the reason for the observed pattern on the strainer made by the beaded pins?

_____

_____

_____

Summary:

This activity is useful in showing where the sun has been during the day in a model sky (the dome-shaped strainer). If you do this at different intervals during the month or the year, then you have a record of where the sun has been in the sky during the year. Students should generally observe that the sun is lower in the sky in the early morning and late afternoon, and it is at its highest point at solar noon. They should also be able to generalize that the sun appears to rise in the east and pass across the sky in an arc from the east to the west and set in the west. The sun is at its highest point when it is in the south. Students should also observe that the sun rises north of east and sets north of west during the spring, summer, and autumn months. The higher the latitude, the more pronounced this becomes. The farthest north of east for a rising sun and north of west for a setting sun would be represented by the summer solstice. The students should also observe that the sun rises and sets almost directly east and west respectively on the spring and autumn equinoxes.

Extensions:

You might use a magnetic compass to determine the relative directions for sunrise, noon, and sunset for your location. You might use this information to consider true north and magnetic north. You will need to consider the time of year and whether you are on standard time or daylight saving time as well.

You may want to measure the angle of the sun at various times of the day. You can use several methods for determining this angle, including having the students build a protractor sextant.

36

Name: _____ Date:_____

STUDENT INQUIRY ACTIVITY 3: SKY DOMES (CONT.)

Assessment:

Have your students make a diagram of the path of the sun across the sky like the one below.

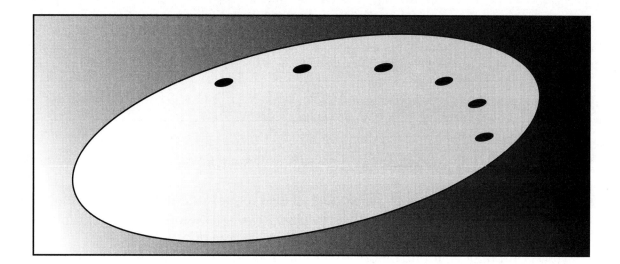

STUDENT INQUIRY ACTIVITY 4: GLOBE ENCOUNTERS OF THE SHADOW KIND

Topic: Daytime Astronomy: Observations of shadows cast by the sun on a globe of the earth.

Science and Mathematics Standards:

NSES: Unifying Concepts and Processes including Systems, Order, and Organization; Evidence, Models, and Explanation; and Constancy, Change, and Measurement. Content Standard A: Inquiry, Content Standard D: Earth and Space Science, and Content Standard G: History and Nature of Science

NCTM: Measurement and Data Analysis and Probability

See **National Standards section** for more details.

Science Concepts:
- A classroom globe can be used to show how the shadows for your location appear on the earth.
- When your city is on top of the globe and the globe is oriented to true north, the globe is facing the same way the earth is, relative to your location.
- The shortest shadow of the day is at solar noon or midday.
- True north may be found by observing and recording a shadow at solar noon.

See **Naive Ideas and Solar System Concepts and Facts section** for more details.

Science Skills:

You will make **observations** of shadows cast by the sun on a globe of the earth. You will make **inferences** about time in other parts of the world based on your observations. You will **manipulate** the globe to make **inferences** about how the shadows and times change as the day and year progress.

See **Science Process Skills section** for descriptions and examples.

Materials: (per group)
A globe of the earth
Coffee can or similar container to support the globe
Small brad or nail
Clay

Content Background:

Students will have made observations of shadows on flat surfaces and will arrive at several inferences relative to the earth-sun relationship. In this activity, students will have an opportunity to observe shadows on a globe and come up with some questions about sunlight and shadows on the earth. They may explore their ideas with globes and artificial light indoors before going outdoors to model shadows on the globe relative to their location on the earth. If oriented correctly, sunlight will strike the globe in a similar way to the way that it strikes Earth.

STUDENT INQUIRY ACTIVITY 4: GLOBE ENCOUNTERS OF THE SHADOW KIND (CONT.)

Students will be able to observe that half of their globe is in the dark, and half is in the light. They will be able to observe approximate areas for sunrise and sunset on their globe, and set up and make predictions about shadows and daylight at various times of the day. Using additional shadow sticks on their setup, they can find areas on the globe that are at midday, sunrise, sunset, etc.

Challenge Question: How does the sun strike the earth right here where I live?

Procedure:
1. Affix a nail with the head as the base to the globe with a piece of clay over your city on the globe.
2. Place the globe in a coffee can. Orient the globe so that your city is on the very top of the globe as it sits in the coffee can. This represents your relative position to the sun for these observations. The nail represents you standing on the earth with the sky overhead.
3. To orient your globe outdoors, it will be important to align north on the globe with north on the earth. It is best to do this at midday. At midday, the shadow will be pointing directly north. With your shadow stick (nail) in place over your location, take your coffee can and globe outside at midday and turn the globe until the North Pole of the globe and the shadow of your nail are aligned. That is, the nail's shadow is pointing at the North Pole on the globe. Midday may be calculated by finding the sunrise and sunset times for the date that you are making your observations in the local newspaper. Example: Suppose sunrise is at 6:17 A.M., and sunset is at 4:38 P.M. (standard time); therefore, the length of the daylight is 10 hours and 21 minutes. The midday point would then be 6:17 A.M. plus 5 hours, 10 minutes (half of the length of daylight), or 11:27 A.M.
4. Students may have already plotted the midday point in the shadow stick activity and determined the direction of true north. If this is the case, they can use that information to set up the globe outside.

STUDENT INQUIRY ACTIVITY 4: GLOBE ENCOUNTERS OF THE SHADOW KIND (CONT.)

Procedure:
1. Affix a nail with the head as the base to the globe with a piece of clay over your city on the globe.
2. Place the globe in a coffee can. Orient the globe so that your city is on the very top of the globe as it sits in the coffee can. This represents your relative position to the sun for these observations. The nail represents you standing on the earth with the sky overhead.
3. To orient your globe outdoors, it will be important to align north on the globe with north on the earth. It is best to do this at midday. At midday, the shadow will be pointing directly north. With your shadow stick (nail) in place over your location, take your coffee can and globe outside at midday and turn the globe until the North Pole of the globe and the shadow of your nail are aligned. That is, the nail's shadow is pointing at the North Pole on the globe.
4. Look at the picture below to see if you have set up your globe correctly.
5. You can place additional nails at other locations on the globe to determine the time of day at those spots.

Exploration/Data Collection:

A. In what direction is your shadow pointing? _____

B. What time is it on your clock? _____

C. Where is the midday sun directly overhead now? _____

D. Is midday east or west of you right now? _____

Name: _____ Date:_____

STUDENT INQUIRY ACTIVITY 4: GLOBE ENCOUNTERS OF THE SHADOW KIND (CONT.)

E. Where on the earth is there no shadow? (a place where the sun is directly overhead)

    _____

F. Where on Earth is the sun setting right now? _____

G. Where on Earth is the sun rising right now? _____

H. Where on Earth is it night right now? _____

I. Where on Earth is it the same time as it is in your location?

    _____

J. Where on Earth will it be midday in one hour? _____

K. Where on Earth was it midday an hour ago? _____

L. What is the shadow like at the equator directly south of your location? (on the same longitude line as your location)

    _____

M. What is the shadow like at the North Pole? _____

N. What is the shadow like at the South Pole? _____

O. What is the shadow like on the Tropic of Cancer directly south of your location? (on the same longitude line as your location)

    _____

P. What is the shadow like at the Tropic of Capricorn? (on the same longitude line as your location)

    _____

Q. If you tape a small card onto the globe adjacent to and north of your shadow stick (nail), you can observe and record the shadow as it moves across the card or globe. Compare your results to the record you kept for Student Inquiry Activities 1 and 2 where you recorded the shadows on the ground.

STUDENT INQUIRY ACTIVITY 4: GLOBE ENCOUNTERS OF THE SHADOW KIND (CONT.)

Assessment: Answers to the Exploration/Data Collection Questions

The answers will vary depending on the location and time of day the observations are made. The following answers are based on observations made in central Illinois in mid-May during the afternoon (daylight saving time).

A. Northeast
B. 2:00 P.M. (DST)
C. Colorado
D. West
E. Just south and west of Mexico City
F. Europe
G. West of Hawaii in the Pacific Ocean
H. Asia
I. Directly north or south
J. Los Angeles
K. Here, since it is daylight saving time, midday was around 1:00 P.M.
L. At the equator, the shadow points southeast and is shorter than here.
M. None observed
N. None observed
O. The shadow points northeast and is much shorter than here.
P. The shadow points southeast and is very long.

STUDENT INQUIRY ACTIVITY 5 : TIME ZONE FINDER

Topic: Daytime Astronomy: The Earth's Rotation and Its Time Zones

Science and Mathematics Standards

NSES: Unifying Concepts and Processes including Systems, Order, and Organization; Evidence, Models, and Explanation; and Constancy, Change, and Measurement. Content Standard A: Inquiry, Content Standard D: Earth and Space Science, and Content Standard G: History and Nature of Science

NCTM: Geometry, Measurement, and Data Analysis and Probability

Note: This activity may also be related to geographic standards supported by the National Council for Social Studies.

See **National Standards section** for more details.

Science Concepts:
- The rotation of the earth in a 24-hour period represents the day.
- The earth is divided by 24 north-south meridians (longitude lines) creating 24 time zones.
- The earth rotates from west to east through time.
- Each time zone is approximately 1,000 miles (1,610 km) wide at the equator.
- Local time may be affected by geographic boundaries, economic trade, and location within a time zone.

See **Naive Ideas and Solar System Concepts and Facts section** for more details.

Science Skills:
You will use a globe of the earth to locate the longitude lines and make **observations** concerning the number of longitude lines on the earth and their relative positions. You will also **observe** the relationship of these lines to the time at various locations on the earth. You will **construct** a time zone finder using a globe and a world atlas or website dealing with time zones. You will use your finder to make **observations** about the time at various locations on the earth.

See **Science Process Skills section** for descriptions and examples.

Materials:
Poster cardstock cut into 3 cm wide x 65 cm long and 10 cm wide x 65 cm long strips
Pencils
Permanent markers
A globe (ideally, one globe per 4 students)*
Tape
Scissors

* The recommended globe size is one with a circumference of 25 inches (63 cm) at the equator.

STUDENT INQUIRY ACTIVITY 5 : TIME ZONE FINDER (CONT.)

Content Background:

The earth rotates once every twenty-four hours, or once a day, on its axis. As we look at a globe's Northern Hemisphere, the rotation is from west to east. The globe is arbitrarily divided into 24 equal parts by longitude lines or meridians running north and south from the North Pole to the South Pole. These lines are 15 degrees apart and converge at the Poles. If you divide 360 degrees by 24 (hours), you see how the separation of each line of longitude or meridian is represented by 15 degrees. The earth has a circumference at the equator that is approximately 24,000 miles (38,640 km). Since the earth rotates through 15 degrees of longitude each hour, you can see that it is spinning at the rate of about 1,000 miles (1,610 km) per hour at the equator.

Time zones are based on the division of the earth into 24 equal parts and are referenced to Greenwich Mean Time at the Prime Meridian in Greenwich, England. UTC or Universal Time Coordinated is calculated from this reference. This may also be referred to as GMT or Greenwich Mean Time. A second meridian, the international date line, is used as a reference for the change of days and is located at 180 degrees from Greenwich. The international date line passes through a sparsely populated area in the Pacific Ocean just east of New Zealand. Time east of the date line is one day earlier, and time west of the date line is one day later. *Example:* If it is 12:00 noon on Sunday in Honolulu, Hawaii, then it is 10:00 A.M. on Monday in Auckland, New Zealand. Auckland is only two time zones to the east of Hawaii, but it is also east of the international date line, so we need to add one day.

The time in any given city on the earth may not necessarily coincide with what you observe on a globe, since local time may be affected by whether your locale observes daylight saving time or may adopt an adjacent time zone's time for convenience. The state of Indiana in the United States does not use daylight saving time in the summer. Most of Indiana is on eastern standard time all year. Gary, Indiana, uses the local time for Chicago (central time) all year for convenience. New Albany, Indiana, uses the local time for Louisville, Kentucky, (eastern time) for convenience. Indiana is on the western edge of the eastern time zone; hence, the actual sunrise is about 56 minutes later in Indianapolis, Indiana, than it is for Boston, Massachusetts, in the same time zone. This explains why Indiana hasn't adopted daylight saving time.

Challenge Question: How can I find the times around the world?

Procedure:

1. Wrap a 10-cm wide band of cardstock around a globe at the equator. Cut the band so that it just fits around the globe and tape it, making a band.
2. While the 10-cm band is wrapped around the globe, mark each of the longitude lines on the band. Label them with the longitude numbers 0 through 180 in each direction from the Prime Meridian. Note that there is only one Prime Meridian (0 degrees) and one international date line (180 degrees). This larger band is the "Earth band."
3. Wrap a second 3-cm band around the first band and mark the longitude lines to match the lines on the first band. Label each of these lines with the twenty-four hours of the day. Tape the ends of this band as in the wide band. The wide band should be free to rotate inside the narrow band. The narrow band represents time and may be referred to as the "time band."

44

STUDENT INQUIRY ACTIVITY 5: TIME ZONE FINDER (CONT.)

4. What you have created is a 10-cm cylinder representing the longitudes or meridians of the earth. These meridians also represent the theoretical time zones for the earth.

5. If you rotate the wide band in a counterclockwise direction inside the narrow "time band," you can approximate the time for each time zone on the earth.

Time Zone Finder I

You will be making a time zone finder like the one above.

Materials:
1, 10-cm wide x 65-cm long cardstock strip
1, 3-cm wide x 65-cm long cardstock strip
A globe of the earth
Tape
Scissors

Procedure:

1. Wrap a 10-cm wide band of cardstock around a globe at the equator. Cut the band so that it just fits around the globe and tape it, making a band.

2. While the 10-cm band is wrapped around the globe, mark each of the longitude lines on the band with a pencil. Label them with the longitude numbers 0 through 180 in each direction from the Prime Meridian. Note there is only one Prime Meridian (0 degrees) and one international date line (180 degrees). This larger band is the "Earth band."

3. Wrap the second 3-cm band around the first band and mark the longitude lines to match the lines on the first band with a pencil. Label each of these lines with the twenty-four hours of the day. *Note:* The time should be labeled in a counterclockwise direction starting with 12 noon, 1 P.M., 2 P.M., 3 P.M., etc.

Name: _____ Date:_____

STUDENT INQUIRY ACTIVITY 5: TIME ZONE FINDER (CONT.)

4. Tape the ends of this band as in the wide band. The larger band should be free to rotate inside the narrow band. The narrow band represents time and may be referred to as the "time band."

5. What you have created is a 10-cm cylinder representing the longitudes or meridians of the earth. These meridians also represent the theoretical time zones for the earth.

6. If you rotate the wide band in a counterclockwise direction inside the narrow "time band," you can approximate the time for each time zone on the earth.

Exploration/Data Collection:

A. Place the narrower "time band" around the globe. Align 12 noon with the 90 degree west longitude line. This line passes near Chicago, Illinois. Answer the following questions, assuming that it is 12 noon in Chicago.

What time do you think it would be in Mexico City? _____

What time do you think it would be in Denver, Colorado? _____

What time do you think it would be in Los Angeles, California? _____

What time do you think it would be in Honolulu, Hawaii? _____

What time do you think it would be in New York, New York? _____

B. Use an atlas or an Internet source such as www.timeanddate.com.Worldclock/ to find the actual times for the cities above and other cities in the world relative to your city or a major city in your time zone, such as Chicago. Use this information to label your time zone finder, or use the table below:

New York	1 P.M.	Jakarta*	1 A.M. (add 1 day)
Chicago	12 noon	Dhaka	12 midnight
Denver	11 A.M.	Karachi*	11 P.M.
Los Angeles	10 A.M.	Tehran	10 P.M.
Anchorage	9 A.M.	Moscow	9 P.M.
Honolulu*	8 A.M.	Cairo	8 P.M.
Midway	7 A.M.	Paris/Rome	7 P.M.
		London	6 P.M.

International Date Line			
Auckland	5 A.M. (add 1 day)		
Sydney*	4 A.M. (add 1 day)		
Tokyo*	3 A.M. (add 1 day)	Buenos Aires*	3 P.M.
Beijing*	2 A.M. (add 1 day)	Halifax	2 P.M.

* Means that the place does not observe daylight saving time in the summer.

Name: _____ Date:_____

STUDENT INQUIRY ACTIVITY 5: TIME ZONE FINDER (CONT.)

Note: If you cross the international date line to the west, you add a day. If you cross the international date line to the east, you subtract a day.

Disclaimer: It is very difficult to say that all of these times are accurate, since state and provincial governments as well as national governing bodies make changes from year to year. It is best to consult websites for current information as we have here. Another source for information concerning time, daylight hours, and other astronomical events is *The Old Farmer's Almanac*, by Robert B. Thomas, which can be found at most newsstands, especially around the first of the year.

C. Place the narrow **"time band"** around the wider **"earth band."** Rotate the earth band counterclockwise while holding the time band still. Note that the earth rotates from west to east (left to right) through time. Use your time zone finder to locate the time for various cities relative to your time zone.

Time Zone Finder II

The time zone finder that you made represents cylinders or bands that were placed over the globe. This same information may be placed on flat discs that may be rotated to find the time in various places on Earth.

Cut out the disc labeled "Earth Wheel" and the one labeled "Time Wheel" on the next two pages. Using a brass fastener, place the two discs together so that the Earth Wheel is on top of the Time Wheel.

To use the time zone finder, rotate the wheel that includes the names of the cities from west to east until the major city for your time zone is aligned with the current hour. Once you have aligned your time, you can determine the time in any other area on the earth by looking at the time aligned with that city.

Exploration/Data Collection:

Set the earth wheel at 12 noon for Chicago, and answer the following questions.

A. What time and day is it in Moscow? _____

B. What time and day is it in Sydney? _____

C. What time and day is it in Honolulu? _____

D. What time and day is it in London? _____

Name: _____ Date:_____

STUDENT INQUIRY ACTIVITY 5: TIME ZONE FINDER (CONT.)

Summary:

What is being observed in this activity is the change in time on the earth relative to the earth's rotation and the organization and standardization of time zones. Generally speaking, time changes by one hour for every 15 degrees of longitude east or west. Local or regional differences in the observed time relative to the expected time in a time zone exist because of geographic location or convenience.

Time is a very important concept, and this activity represents another example of how time is measured relative to the rotation of the earth and regions of longitude.

Real-World Application:

Understanding time and the differences that exist is very important when we are traveling or communicating with someone in another part of the world. Understanding how time and date are determined allows you to predict relatively accurately the time anywhere in the world. Additionally, understanding the system of time zones and the relationship of time to the earth's rotation is information about the order that exists in our solar system.

Earth Wheel

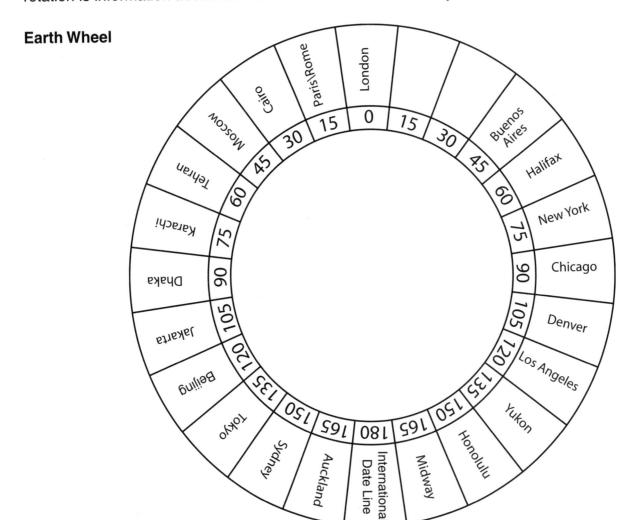

Name: _____ Date:_____

STUDENT INQUIRY ACTIVITY 5: TIME ZONE FINDER (CONT.)

Time Wheel

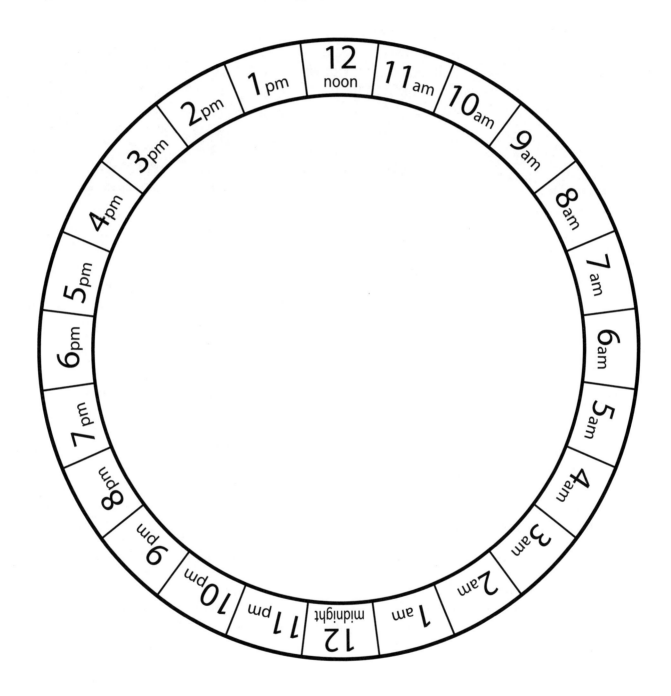

STUDENT INQUIRY ACTIVITY 6: MEASURING THE SUN'S LOCATION

Topic: Daytime Astronomy: Determining the exact position of the sun in the sky relative to your position on the earth

> **Science and Mathematics Standards:**
>
> **NSES:** Unifying Concepts and Processes including Systems, Order, and Organization; Evidence, Models, and Explanation; and Constancy, Change, and Measurement. Content Standard A: Inquiry, Content Standard D: Earth and Space Science, and Content Standard G: History and Nature of Science
>
> **NCTM:** Geometry, Measurement, and Data Analysis and Probability
>
> See **National Standards section** for more details.

Science Concepts:
- The sun appears to move across the sky in an east-west direction due to the earth's actual rotation from west to east.
- The altitude of the sun increases during the hours before midday, reaches a maximum altitude near midday, and then decreases after midday. Note that midday is not necessarily noon, relative to "clock time." Midday may be defined as the time when the sun is at its highest point in the sky, and a shadow cast by the sun points directly north on any given day.
- The sun's position in the sky at any one time changes from one day to the next.

See **Naive Ideas and Solar System Concepts and Facts section** for more details.

Science Skills:
You will make **observations** of the sun's locations during periods of the same day and different days. You will also be able to make **predictions** of the sun's location in the sky from day to day based on your **analysis** of the data collected. You will **collect** and **record data measurements** of shadows caused by the sun. You will **interpret** and **analyze** collected data and make **generalized statements** as to the sun's motions.

See **Science Process Skills section** for descriptions and examples.

Content Background:
The earth rotates on its axis once every day. This rotation from west to east causes the sun to appear to move across the sky from east to west. As the sun appears to rise in the east, move across the sky, and set in the west, the exact position of the sun may be measured quite accurately with a very simple device.

To pinpoint the location of the sun, two measurements are required; the **altitude** of the sun, or the number of degrees above the horizon, and the **azimuth** of the sun, or the position of the sun above a certain point on the horizon. The horizon may be divided into 360 parts, one part for each degree of the horizon. If you are facing north, then your azimuth is zero (0) degrees. The azimuth for east is 90 degrees, 180 degrees for south, and 270 degrees is west. The sun's location can be established in terms of azimuth and altitude.

STUDENT INQUIRY ACTIVITY 6: MEASURING THE SUN'S LOCATION

Twice a year, the sun will rise and set directly east and west. These two occasions are the **vernal equinox** and **autumnal equinox**. Following the vernal equinox (in March), the sun will rise a little farther to the north each day until the summer solstice (in June) is reached. The sun will then begin to rise (and set) farther to the south until the winter solstice is reached in December. Following the winter solstice, the sun begins to rise (and set) farther to the north each morning.

As the sun rises (and sets) farther on the southern horizon, the sun will also appear lower in the southern sky. The converse is also true, as the sun rises (and sets) along the northern horizon, the sun will appear higher in the sky. This change in the altitude of the sun is most noticeable at noon when the sun will appear highest in the sky on the meridian, or an imaginary line running from north to south directly above the observer.

Materials:

Wood block (approximately 18 cm x 12 cm)	Hammer
Protractor	Glue
Photocopy of an actual protractor	Ruler
Nail, 2.0–2.5 cm length	Blank paper
Nail, 1.0 cm length	
Thumbtack	

Challenge Questions: How does the position of the sun change during the day? How does the position of the sun change with the different seasons?

Procedure:

Note: The Sun Location Measurement Device (SLMD) is a slightly modified version of the ARIES SunTracker that was developed as part of the Project Aries (Astronomy Resources for Intercurricular Elementary Science) *Module Two: Astronomy I: Thinking About the Earth and the Sun* by Marvin C. Grossman, Irwin I. Shaprio, and R. Bruce Ward, Harvard University, 1997.

A. Building the Sun Location Measurement Device (SLMD)

The Sun Location Measurement Device is composed of two pieces. A compass rose, similar to those found on maps, is needed for the SLMD to be correctly placed, and the Sun Location Measurement Device (SLMD) will also be constructed.

To make a compass rose, draw two perpendicular line segments that intersect at their midpoints on a piece of paper. For accuracy in determining the azimuth, each line segment should be approximately 10 centimeters, or a little longer than one-half the length of the SLMD. Designate one end of one of the line segments as North and label this 0 degrees. In a clockwise direction, label each of the other 3 ends of the segments as East, 90 degrees; South, 180 degrees; and West, 270 degrees. Next, using a protractor, draw segments representing each 10-degree interval around the compass rose (10, 20, 30, ... degrees). (See Figure 1.)

STUDENT INQUIRY ACTIVITY 6 : MEASURING THE SUN'S LOCATION

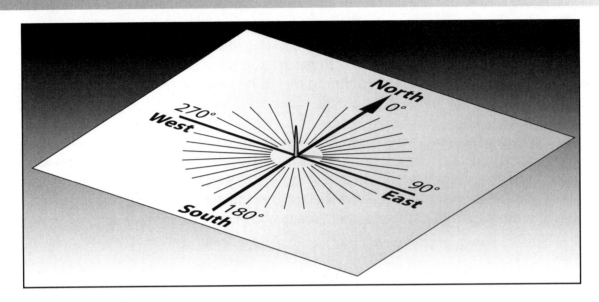

Figure 1

To construct the Sun Location Measurement Device (SLMD), you need to first obtain a paper protractor. This can be done by photocopying any ordinary protractor. A protractor that is approximately 15 cm long by 10 cm high is suggested. Next, trim the paper copy of the protractor to fit onto the side of a one-inch board. The length and width of the board needs to be large enough to accommodate the paper protractor. Sand the board to remove all splinters and rough edges. After the board is sanded, the dust is removed, and the paper protractor is trimmed, glue the paper protractor onto the board. Align the protractor so the line segment from 0 degrees to 180 degrees is parallel to the top edge of the board, and the 90 degrees of the protractor is toward the bottom of the board. (See Figure 2.)

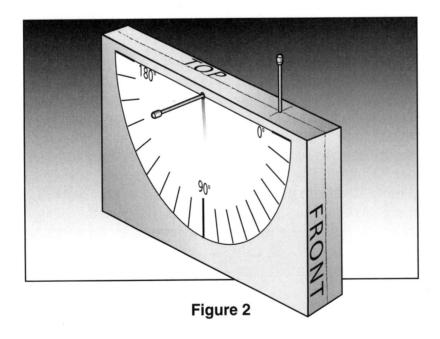

Figure 2

52

STUDENT INQUIRY ACTIVITY 6: MEASURING THE SUN'S LOCATION

On the top edge of the board, draw a line running through the center and the entire length of the board. Do the same along one of the side edges of the board. This side edge will be considered the front of the Sun Location Measurement Device (SLMD). On the top edge of the SLMD, hammer a 2.0–2.5 cm nail located about one-third along the length of the board. This nail should not be hammered completely in but left with about 2 cm of length still exposed. Be careful to place this nail directly on the line drawn on the board, and be sure the nail is straight up and down and perpendicular to the drawn line on the top edge of the board. On the protractor side of the piece of wood at the vertex of the two 90-degree angles forming the protractor, hammer the 1.0 cm nail approximately halfway into the board. In the center of the bottom edge of the SLMD, make a small hole with a nail slightly larger than a thumbtack by hammering in the nail and then removing it. (See Figure 2.)

In the center of the compass rose, push a thumbtack through the compass rose from the back to the front. Now place the wooden SLMD on the compass rose so that the thumbtack enters the nail hole on the bottom of the SLMD. The SLMD should sit on the compass rose and rotate freely.

B. To Use the Sun Location Measurement Device (SLMD)

Place the compass rose in a sunny location that is smooth and level, and then place the wooden block (SLMD) on top of the compass rose.

Step 1. Using a magnetic compass, align the compass rose so 0 degrees or North points towards magnetic north.

Step 2. Without moving the compass rose, turn the SLMD until the front of the device is facing the sun.

Step 3. Continue to rotate the SLMD until the shadow of the nail on top of the SLMD aligns with the line drawn on top of the block. To determine the azimuth of the sun, read the number of degrees that aligns with the line on the front of the SLMD.

Step 4. In this position, the nail on the side of the SLMD should be casting its shadow on the protractor. This reading represents the altitude of the sun. (*Note:* Depending on the length of this nail, the SLMD may have to be tilted very slightly to cast a shadow on the protractor. If this is necessary, be sure not to change the azimuth position.

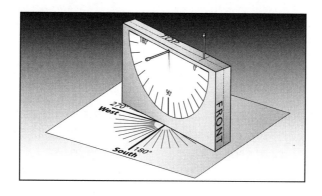

Name: _____ Date:_____

STUDENT INQUIRY ACTIVITY 6: MEASURING THE SUN'S LOCATION

Exploration/Data Collection:
1. Use the SLMD to determine the sun's azimuth and altitude at different times of the day. Record your readings in the table below. Additional readings may be recorded on your own paper.

Date	Time	Azimuth	Altitude

2. Study your data. What patterns do you see in the azimuth?

_____

_____

3. What patterns do you see in the altitude?

_____

_____

Conclusions:
1. Based on your data and observations, make a general statement about the daily changes in the position of the sun.

_____

_____

2. Based on your data and observations, make a general statement about the seasonal changes in the position of the sun.

_____

_____

Summary:
   While using the Sun Location Measurement Device, students will discover that a very simple device can provide very accurate information. The data collected by the students should reveal that the sun's altitude increases from 0 degrees at sunrise to a maximum at midday and then decreases to 0 degrees at sunset. The data will also reveal that in the Northern Hemi-

Name: _____ Date:_____

STUDENT INQUIRY ACTIVITY **6**: MEASURING THE SUN'S LOCATION

sphere, the sun's azimuth increases during the day from a minimum azimuth at sunrise to a maximum azimuth at sunset. Further analysis of the data will demonstrate that the sun rises farther north along the eastern horizon from the vernal equinox until the summer solstice. Once reaching its northernmost point along the eastern horizon, the sun will then begin to appear farther south on the eastern horizon each day until the winter solstice, at which time it will begin to appear farther north on the eastern horizon each morning. Similar movement will be noted in regard to the sun's position on the western horizon during sunsets.

Specific data as to the position of the sun may be obtained from a number of Internet references such as: *Sun or Moon Altitude/Azimuth Table for One Day* at aa.usno.navy.mil/data/docs/AltAz.html; *Sun, Moon and Earth Applet* at www.jgiesen.de/SME/; or a software program such as: *SkyGazer, A Guide to the Heavens* published by Carina Software.

Extensions:

Students could investigate the position of the sun at the same time but on different days of the year. Students in different locations could collect data about the position of the sun and share their data with students in other locations via the Internet.

Real-World Applications:

The position of the sun is important in the consideration of the development and construction of buildings. Designers will take into consideration how homes and buildings will be exposed to the sunlight for heating and cooling purposes. Landscapers also consider the sun's position as decisions about the location of vegetation, trees, bushes, and so on around homes are being made.

Assessments: Answers to Exploration/Data Collection Questions

2. What patterns do you see in the azimuth?

    Students' responses should indicate the sun rising farther northward on the eastern horizon from the vernal equinox (March 20–22) until the summer solstice (June 21–22). After the occurrence of the summer solstice, the sun will rise farther south on the eastern horizon until the winter solstice (December 21–22) when the sun will again begin to rise farther to the north. Students' responses might also note that on the vernal equinox and autumn equinox (September 20–22), the sun will rise and set on the horizon directly east and west, respectively.

    Students' measurements may be checked for accuracy by comparing their data to data collected by the instructor or to data obtained via another accepted resource.

3. What patterns do you see in the altitude?

    Students' responses should mention the fact that the sun will appear higher in the sky during the summer months and lower in the sky during the winter months. Explanations that might further be included are that the sun will be at its maximum altitude near midday on the summer solstice and at its minimum altitude near midday on the winter solstice.

STUDENT INQUIRY ACTIVITY **7** : OBSERVING THE MOON'S PHASES

Topic: The Sun, Moon, and Planets: Phases of the Moon

Science and Mathematics Standards:

NSES: Unifying Concepts and Processes including Systems, Order, and Organization; Evidence, Models, and Explanation; and Constancy, Change, and Measurement; Content Standard A: Inquiry, Content Standard D: Earth and Space Science, and Content Standard G: History and Nature of Science

NCTM: Measurement and Data Analysis and Probability

See **National Standards section** for additional information.

Science Concepts:
- The moon goes through daily changes or phases as it orbits the earth.
- The moon rises about 50 minutes later each day.
- The moon's phases are a result of the moon being round and the fact that the angle that it makes with the earth and the sun changes during its orbit.
- The moon appears to travel from east to west across the southern sky at night in the Northern Hemisphere of the earth.
- The same side of the moon is always toward the earth because the moon rotates at the same rate that it revolves around the earth.
- The moon has a near side and a far side relative to the earth. We cannot see the far side from the earth's vantage point.
- All sides of the moon are illuminated as it orbits the earth. When the moon is in its new moon phase, the far side of the moon is illuminated. Hence, the moon does not have a permanent dark side and a permanent light side.
- A winter full moon is higher in the sky than a summer full moon.
- A new moon can eclipse the sun, and its shadow covers a small portion of the earth.

See **Naive Ideas and Solar System Concepts and Facts section** for additional information.

Science Skills:

Students will **predict** the relative sizes of the moon phases. Students will also do extended **observations** of the nighttime sky where they will **measure** the position of the moon and changes in positions of the moon from one observation period to the next. Students will **model** the changing moon phases with a light source and rubber ball.

See **Science Process Skills section** for additional information.

Content Background:

Daily observations of the moon reveal a slight change in the moon's appearance from one day to the next. These changes are due to the rotation of the moon around the earth and the earth's rotation around the sun. These changes are known as the phases of the moon. The

STUDENT INQUIRY ACTIVITY **7** : OBSERVING THE MOON'S PHASES (CONT.)

four most common phases are **new moon**, **full moon**, **first quarter**, and **third (or last) quarter**. A new moon occurs when the moon lines up between the sun and the earth, and a full moon occurs when the earth is between the sun and the moon. It requires 29.5 days for the moon to cycle through all its phases. During the lunar cycle, the observer on the earth always sees the same side of the moon. This phenomenon occurs because the moon rotates on its axis at the same rate that the moon revolves around the earth. Phases of the moon other than new, full, first quarter, and third quarter phases are identified by their shapes and how they are changing. If the moon as it appears from Earth is less than one-half illuminated, then it is called a **crescent moon**. If the moon appears greater than one-half illuminated, then the moon is known as a **gibbous moon**. A moon whose appearance is increasing in size is known as a **waxing moon**, while a moon appearing to get smaller in size is called a **waning moon**. By combining these terms, a moon may be termed waxing crescent, waxing gibbous, waning crescent, or waning gibbous. Each quarter phase is approximately one week apart.

Other Facts About the Moon:
- The moon is Earth's natural satellite.
- The moon orbits the earth about once a month, or every 27.3 days.
- The moon is 239,000 miles (384,000 km) from the earth.
- The moon's diameter is 2,160 miles (3,476 km).
- The moon's gravity is 1/6 that of Earth.
- The moon's gravity causes tides in the earth's oceans.

Materials:
Light source, such as floor lamp or clamp-on light with a 100–200 watt light bulb
Small white ball, approximately 3–5 inches in diameter. (A smooth ball works best, although a rough Styrofoam ball may also work. Colored rubber balls may also be spray-painted with white spray paint to create white balls.)
Copy paper

Challenge Questions: Why does the appearance of the moon change?
How does the moon's appearance change daily?

Procedure:

Part A – Observing the Changing Moon
Classroom Discussion:

Begin the discussion by asking the students how many of them have ever observed the moon. Ask them if they know how the moon's appearance changes and why. Ask the students to predict how much of their hand would be needed when held at arm's-length to cover the full moon.

1. Research when the next new moon will occur. (Your daily newspaper may carry this information, it may be on a calendar, check with an astronomy organization, or visit www.stardate.org or a similar website for this information.)

STUDENT INQUIRY ACTIVITY 7: OBSERVING THE MOON'S PHASES (CONT.)

2. Because a new moon is not visible, observe the shape and location of the observable moon on the evening following the new moon. On a horizontal sheet of copy paper, draw your observation. Record the day's date and time next to your drawing. The distance of the moon above the horizon may be measured in terms of hands or fists and/or fingers' widths. To measure using your hands, extend both hands at full arm's-length and make a fist. Starting with one fist just touching the horizon, measure the number of fists required to reach the moon. Width of fingers may be used for any distances that are less than one full fist.

3. Continue to observe, measure, and record the moon's location on each clear night for the next 2–3 weeks.

Conclusions:

1. What conclusions can you draw about how the moon's appearance changes each evening?

_____

_____

_____

2. How much of the student's hand, when held at full arm's-length, is needed to cover the moon?

_____

_____

_____

Part B – Demonstrating the Moon's Phases

1. This demonstration must be conducted in a dark or nearly dark room with lights off and window shades drawn. Place a single light source containing a 100–200 watt light bulb in the center of the room. Students will form a large circle around the light source with each student standing at least 1.5 to 2 arm's-lengths from each other. Each student should have a round white ball.

STUDENT INQUIRY ACTIVITY **7** : OBSERVING THE MOON'S PHASES (CONT.)

2. The light source in the center of the room represents the sun, and the white ball in each student's hand represents the moon. The student's head represents the earth. You may also think of the eyes representing an observer on Earth. Begin with the students facing the sun (light source). Explain to them that their head represents the earth and that their eyes are observing the moon as it would appear from the earth. Instruct the students to hold the moon (white ball) in front of them with their left hand extended as they face

the sun. The moon should not block the sunlight but be held slightly above their line of sight to the sun.

3. This is the new moon phase. On a piece of paper, have the students draw a circle. This circle represents the moon that they are observing. Darken the part of the circle (moon) that is not illuminated. Also have the students draw the location of the sun, Earth, and moon as if they were above the room looking down into the room. (See sample below.)

New Moon — Sun

4. While holding the moon (white ball) in their left hand in front of them, have the students rotate, or turn, 90 degrees to their left. This is the first quarter moon phase. Have the students draw a second circle. Darken the part of the moon that is not illuminated. Again have the students draw and label the view of a first quarter moon as seen from above.

5. While holding the moon (white ball) in their left hand in front of them, have the students rotate or turn another 90 degrees to their left. (They should now have the light source directly behind them and the moon directly opposite the light source.) If necessary, have the students hold the moon high enough to be fully illuminated by the light source. This represents the full moon phase. Have the students draw a third circle. They should darken the part of the moon that is not illuminated sand draw and label the view from above.

Name: _____ Date:_____

STUDENT INQUIRY ACTIVITY 7: OBSERVING THE MOON'S PHASES (CONT.)

6. Have the students switch the moon (white ball) to their right hand and hold it in front of them, and then have them rotate or turn another 90 degrees to their left. This is the third quarter moon phase. Have the students draw a fourth circle. Darken the part of the moon that is not illuminated and draw and label the view from above.

7. While holding the moon (white ball) in their right hand in front of them, have the students turn another 90 degrees to their left. They should now have rotated back to the new moon phase.

8. Beginning in the new moon phase and holding the moon in their left hand in front of them, have the students slowly rotate from the new moon phase to the first quarter phase. The crescent moon that students observe between the new and first quarter phase is called a waxing crescent moon. Have the students draw a circle. Darken the part of the moon that is not illuminated. A moon's phase that is less than half illuminated is referred to as a crescent moon. If the crescent moon is getting larger, it is known as a waxing crescent. If the crescent moon is getting smaller, it is known as a waning crescent moon.

9. Now have the students slowly move from the first quarter moon phase to the full moon phase. The larger than half moon that students observe between the first quarter moon and full moon is called a waxing gibbous moon. Have the students draw a circle. Darken the part of the moon that is not illuminated. A moon's phase that is more than half illuminated is referred to as a gibbous moon. If the gibbous moon is getting larger, it is known as a waxing gibbous moon. If the gibbous moon is getting smaller, it is known as a waning gibbous moon.

10. Have the students draw a circle. Have the students darken the part of the moon that is not illuminated between the full moon and third quarter phases. What is the name of this moon?

    _____

11. Have the students draw a circle, and then have them darken the part of the moon that is not illuminated between the third quarter and new moon phases. What is the name of this moon?

    _____

12. Have the students make at least one observation of the moon using the following technique. Use a paper punch to make a hole in a piece of paper. Take the paper outside and observe the moon through the punched hole. How large does the moon appear to be, relative to the punched hole?

    _____

Name: _____ Date:_____

STUDENT INQUIRY ACTIVITY 7: OBSERVING THE MOON'S PHASES (CONT.)

Summary:

Students should discover that when starting with the new moon, on each subsequent evening, the illuminated portion of the moon appears a little larger until reaching the full moon phase over a two-week period. Following the full moon, students should discover that the illuminated portion of the moon appears to get slightly smaller each day until returning to the new moon phase. Students may also observe that when observing the moon at the same time each night, the moon will appear a little farther to the east than the previous evening's location.

Students will discover that the full moon will appear to be the same size as a paper punch hole in a piece of paper.

Extensions:

Students could make early morning observations of the moon and note the time the moon rises and any changes in the moon's appearance.

Real-World Applications:

Students will find that the phase of the moon gradually changes each day. Some days the moon will not be visible. Students will also discover that while the sun is many times greater in size than the moon, both the sun and moon will appear to be the same size in the sky. This phenomenon is best illustrated by a solar eclipse when the moon blocks the sun. Awareness of the moon should be heightened through these activities, encouraging students to ask additional questions about the moon. For instance, they may want to research the concept of tides in the oceans on the earth and the relationship of daily tide changes to the position and phases of the moon. During this research, they should also learn that tides are the result of the gravitational pull of the earth, moon, and sun and the interaction of the gravity of all three heavenly bodies.

Assessments:
Part A – Observing the Changing Moon: Conclusions

1. Students' observations should show that each evening the size of the illuminated moon becomes a little larger, increasing in size from a small crescent shape on the right-hand side of the moon to a moon whose entire right half is illuminated (called a first quarter moon). Observations should continue to show from the first quarter moon the left-hand side of the moon becoming more illuminated until the entire moon is illuminated (called a full moon).

   Further observations past the full moon phase will reveal the right-hand side of the moon gradually getting smaller or less illuminated. As this occurs, the left-hand side of the moon becomes fully illuminated, representing the third quarter.

2. Only the end of the thumb is needed to cover the moon.

61

STUDENT INQUIRY ACTIVITY 7: OBSERVING THE MOON'S PHASES (CONT.)

Part B – Demonstrating the Moon's Phases

3. Each student's drawing of a new moon should be a circle that is completely dark because no sunlight can reach the side of the moon facing the earth and be reflected to the earth.

4. In the first quarter moon phase, the right-hand side of the moon is illuminated, and the left-hand side of the moon is dark. The light from the sun (light source) is striking the right-hand side of the moon (white ball) and being reflected to the earth.

5. In the full moon phase, the entire side of the moon that faces the earth is illuminated by the sun (light source), and the light is reflected to the earth.

6. In the third quarter moon phase, the left-hand side of the moon is illuminated, and the right-hand side of the moon is dark.

8. Each student's drawing of a waxing crescent moon should be a circle with a small crescent (less than half) of the right-hand side of the moon illuminated and the rest of the moon darkened.

9. Each student's drawing of a waxing gibbous moon should be a circle with over half of the moon illuminated, and only a small crescent segment on the left-hand side of the moon darkened.

10. For the waning gibbous moon, each student's drawing should show more than half of the left-hand side of the moon illuminated with just a small crescent segment on the right-hand side of the moon darkened.

11. For the waning crescent moon, the student's drawing should show just a small crescent on the left-hand side of the moon illuminated, the rest of the moon should be shaded dark.

12. The full moon will appear to be the same size as a paper punch hole in a piece of paper.

STUDENT INQUIRY ACTIVITY 8: THOSE BEAUTIFUL ECLIPSES

Topic: The Sun, Moon, and Planets: Lunar and Solar Eclipses

Science and Mathematics Standards:

NSES: Unifying Concepts and Processes including Systems, Order, and Organization; Evidence, Models, and Explanation; and Constancy, Change, and Measurement; Content Standard A: Inquiry, Content Standard D: Earth and Space Science, and Content Standard G: History and Nature of Science

NCTM: Measurement and Data Analysis and Probability

See **National Standards section** for more details.

Science Concepts:

Students will learn how lunar and solar eclipses occur. Students will learn how to model lunar and solar eclipses. Students will understand that lunar and solar eclipses are predictable. The alignment of the earth, moon, and sun is responsible for eclipses.

See **Naive Ideas and Solar System Concepts and Facts section** for more details.

Science Skills:

You will **model** lunar and solar eclipses. Using the model, you will make **observations** of the motions of the earth, moon, and sun. You will also be able to **predict** when it is possible for lunar and solar eclipses to occur, relative to the orbit of the moon about the earth and the earth about the sun.

See **Science Process Skills section** for descriptions and examples.

Content Background:

An **eclipse** is when one celestial body moves into the shadow of another celestial body and is either partially or totally obscured by it. If you walk into the shadow cast by a tree or similar object, then to an observer you have been eclipsed by that tree. That is, the tree has blocked the sunlight that would have reached you and reflected off your body; the tree has come between you and the sun. As the earth revolves around the sun and the moon about the earth, they occasionally align so the sunlight is blocked. When these alignments occur, an eclipse of either the sun or the moon may occur. If the moon blocks the light from the sun resulting in the total disappearance or partial disappearance of the sun as viewed from the earth, then a **solar eclipse** takes place. A **lunar eclipse** occurs when the earth blocks the sun's light from reaching the moon. A solar eclipse is possible when the moon is in its new moon phase and a lunar eclipse is possible when the moon is in its full moon phase. However, eclipses do not occur every time there is a new moon or full moon. The reason for this is because the moon and Earth do not revolve in the same geometric plane each month or year. The earth-moon orbit is approximately six degrees out of alignment with the earth-sun orbit; hence, an eclipse can only occur if these orbital planes intersect during a new moon or full moon phase.

STUDENT INQUIRY ACTIVITY 8: THOSE BEAUTIFUL ECLIPSES (CONT.)

With the present understanding of the motion of the sun, Earth, and moon, the occurrences of solar and lunar eclipses are now predictable. A number of Internet websites, such as http://sunearth.gsfc.nasa.gov/eclipse/eclipse.html, list the times and dates for these upcoming events.

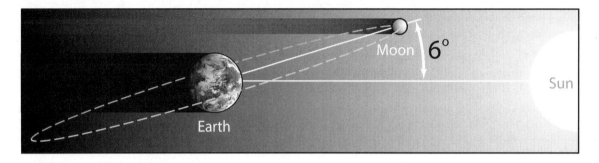

Because light rays travel in straight lines, light from the sun will cause the shadow of the earth or moon to be cone-shaped. The shadow's cone will have two parts: a lighter outer region of the shadow called the **penumbra** and a darker inner region called the **umbra**. During a solar eclipse, the penumbra will cast a shadow covering a length of about 6,400 km (3,977 miles). Individuals in this area will be able to see a partial solar eclipse. The inner shadow, or umbra, will cast a narrower shadow of about 270 km (168 miles) wide, where observers will be treated to a total solar eclipse. An **annular solar eclipse** occurs when the moon orbit is farthest from the earth. The moon passes in front of the sun, but the moon does not totally cover the sun's surface, leaving a ring of sunlight around the moon.

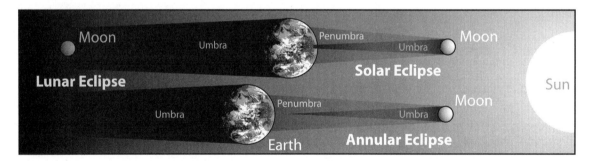

Materials:
Light source, such as a floor lamp or clamp-on light with a 100–200 watt light bulb
Small white ball, approximately 3-5 inches in diameter. (A smooth ball works best, although a rough Styrofoam ball may also work. Colored rubber balls may also be sprayed with white paint to create an adequate reflecting surface.)

Challenge Question: What causes a lunar or solar eclipse?

Procedure:
During the earlier activity, "Observing the Moon's Phases," students demonstrated how the phases of the moon were created. In this activity, students will demonstrate a solar eclipse and a lunar eclipse.

Name: _____ Date:_____

STUDENT INQUIRY ACTIVITY 8: THOSE BEAUTIFUL ECLIPSES (CONT.)

During the simulation of the new moon phase, students faced the sun (light bulb) and held the rubber ball between the sun and the earth with the rubber ball slightly above the plane between the sun and the student's eyes. To demonstrate a solar eclipse during a new moon phase, have the students hold the rubber ball in a direct line with the sun and the student's eyes. The ball should block the light traveling from the sun (light bulb) to the student's eyes. This represents a solar eclipse, since the sun's light was blocked out by the moon. In this demonstration, the student's head represents the earth with the eyes being observers on the earth, the ball represents the moon, and the burning light bulb represents the sun.

Exploration/Data Collection:

1. During what moon phase does a solar eclipse take place?

    _____

2. Look across the room at another student who is demonstrating a solar eclipse. Onto what part of their body is the shadow of the rubber ball (moon) falling?

    _____

3. If there were an insect on the student's shoulder (the same student as in the previous question), would the insect on the student's shoulder be observing a solar eclipse also? Explain your answer.

    _____

    _____

    _____

Name: _____ Date:_____

STUDENT INQUIRY ACTIVITY 8 : THOSE BEAUTIFUL ECLIPSES (CONT.)

4. Why do you think you do not experience a solar eclipse every month?

    _____

    _____

    _____

5. A lunar eclipse occurs during a full moon phase. In the space below, draw the positions of the sun, Earth, and moon during a full moon phase.

    ```




    ```

6. During the activity in which you demonstrated the phases of the moon, you were instructed to hold the rubber ball (moon) above your head and in front of you as you viewed the full moon phase. Why do you think you were instructed to hold the ball above your head?

    _____

    _____

    _____

7. Begin in the first quarter or waxing gibbous moon phase position. Describe what happens to the moon if you hold the moon at eye level and rotate to the full moon phase position.

    _____

    _____

    _____

8. This phenomenon is called a lunar eclipse. Write a definition for a lunar eclipse.

    _____

    _____

    _____

    _____

STUDENT INQUIRY ACTIVITY 8: THOSE BEAUTIFUL ECLIPSES (CONT.)

9. If there were an insect on your shoulder or anywhere below your shoulder, would the insect also observe the lunar eclipse in the same way and same time as you are observing the eclipse?

_____

_____

Conclusions:

10. Make a generalization statement about the number of people on Earth who could view a solar eclipse or lunar eclipse at any one moment. Explain your answer.

_____

_____

_____

_____

Summary:

Eclipses are predictable events and spectacular to observe. Lunar eclipses are more frequent to observe because more people can observe a lunar eclipse when it occurs. Solar eclipses are less observable because a smaller number of people will be in the path of the eclipse when it occurs. Solar eclipses are also more dangerous to observe because of the intensity of the sunlight. To prevent blindness, solar eclipses should be observed either through an indirect method or through approved solar eclipse filters.

Extensions:

Students could research the dates and locations of upcoming eclipses during their lifetime.

Real-World Applications:

Students should understand the dangers in observing a solar eclipse. Because of the intensity of the small area of sunlight, blindness can occur if students attempt to observe a solar eclipse directly. The safest method of observing a solar eclipse is the indirect method. Make a pinpoint in a piece of cardboard that measures approximately 30 centimeters square. With the student's back to the sun, hold the cardboard so as to allow the sunlight to pass through the pinhole. Hold a piece of white paper under the cardboard so the light passing through the pinhole is

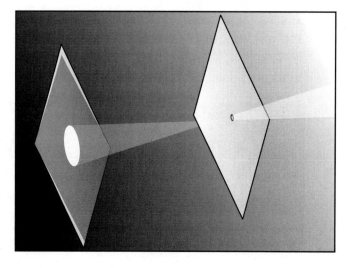

Name: _____ Date:_____

STUDENT INQUIRY ACTIVITY 8: THOSE BEAUTIFUL ECLIPSES (CONT.)

projected onto the white piece of paper. By adjusting the distance that the paper is from the cardboard, the student will be able to project an image of the sun onto the paper and observe the sun as it is eclipsed. (See illustration on previous page.)

Because the light of a lunar eclipse is sunlight reflected off of the moon, a lunar eclipse is safe to observe with the naked eye.

Assessment: Answers to Exploration/Data Collection and Conclusion Questions
1. A solar eclipse can occur only during a new moon phase.
2. The shadow of the moon (rubber ball) will be covering just the eyes of the student across the room.
3. An insect on the shoulder of the student would not be observing the solar eclipse. Because of the distance of the sun and the relative size of the moon, the shadow cast by the moon is too narrow to cover both the observer's eyes and shoulder. Therefore, the light from the sun to the eyes would be blocked, but not the light from the sun to the shoulders.
4. Students' answers will vary but should include some statement(s) about the fact that the sun, Earth, and moon do not orbit in the same plane. Complete understanding of this concept would be demonstrated by stating that the orbit plane containing the earth and moon is about six degrees out of alignment with the sun-earth orbit's plane; therefore, the solar eclipse only occurs when those two planes intersect in the new moon phase position.
5. By holding the moon above the student's head, the moon received all of the light from the sun and was not shaded by the student's head.
6. With the moon at eye level, the moon moves into the full moon phase position and becomes darker as it moves into the shadow of the earth.
7. As you turn to the left, the shadow of the earth (your head) covers more of the moon until it is completely shaded in the full moon phase.
8. Students' answers will vary. Student definitions might infer that a lunar eclipse takes place when the moon moves into the shade of the earth during a full moon phase.
9. Yes, anyone on the dark side of the earth, or the side away from the sun, would be able to see a lunar eclipse.
10. A solar eclipse is visible to just a relatively small number of people because the area on the surface of the earth that is shaded by the moon during the solar eclipse is small. Meanwhile, anyone on the side of the earth away from the sun will be able to observe the lunar eclipse. Therefore, lunar eclipses appear to be more common than a solar eclipse.

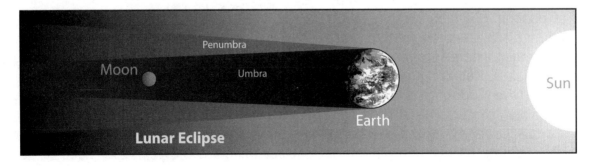

Inquiry Activity **9**: Scaling the Solar System

Topic: The Sun, Moon, and Planets: Modeling the distance the planets are located from the sun.

Science Concepts:

- Our solar system consists of the sun, nine planets and their satellites, the asteroids, comets, and meteors.
- The planets of our solar system vary greatly in their distance from the sun; however, the first four planets, Mercury, Venus, Earth, and Mars, are relatively evenly spaced with the following rough proportional distance from the sun: If Mercury represents a distance of 1 unit from the sun, than Venus is roughly 2 units, Earth 3 units, and Mars 4 units from the sun. (See the actual distances in the table on page 71.) The distance to Jupiter based on this scale would be roughly 12 units from the sun or 3 times the distance of Mars from the sun. Saturn would be represented by 24 units, Uranus 48 units, Neptune about 78 units, and Pluto 102 units.
- The distance that a planet is located from the sun is one factor that determines the planet's characteristics.
- All of the planets orbit around the sun in the same direction, and their orbits are all in a similar plane. If you made a model of the solar system in which the sun and the planets were all floating in water, you would have a fairly accurate picture of their relationship. Pluto's orbit is slightly eccentric in that its orbit is more elliptical and askew of the plane of orbit for the other planets.

See **Naive Ideas and Solar System Concepts and Facts section** for more details.

Science Skills:

Students will **measure** the distance from the sun to the planets of the solar system. Students will **research** and **analyze** the different characteristics and features of the planets of the solar system.

See **Science Process Skills section** for descriptions and examples.

Inquiry Activity 9 : Scaling the Solar System (cont.)

Content Background:

The solar system is defined as the sun and all of the objects revolving around the sun. In addition to the nine planets, these objects include all the moons of the planets, asteroids, comets, meteorites and meteors, and all of the dust and particles that are attracted by the sun's gravity. Our solar system is in just one of an estimated fifty billion galaxies in the universe. Pluto, which is about 5.87 billion kilometers (3.7 billion miles) from the sun, is the most distant object known in our solar system. The nine planets orbiting the sun move in elliptical and not perfectly circular orbits. While the elliptical orbits result in a small variation of the sun-to-planet distance, the variation is only a small fraction of their total distance from the sun. For example, the mean distance for the sun-to-Earth is 149.6 million kilometers (93 million miles). This distance may vary by approximately 2.5 million kilometers (1.6 million miles), which is a rather insignificant 1.7%. Contrary to what many students believe, the Earth is actually closer to the sun during winter than during the summer. The reason that summer months are warmer than winter months has little to do with the distance from the sun. It occurs because during the summer months, the earth's North Pole is tilted towards the sun, and during the winter, the North Pole is pointed away from the sun.

The planets of the solar system may be classified into two types: terrestrial and gaseous planets. Mercury, Venus, Earth, and Mars are considered terrestrial planets because they are composed of solid rock surfaces. Jupiter, Saturn, Uranus, and Neptune are called gaseous planets because they have no solid surfaces on which to stand. Pluto appears to be a solid planet with an outer layer of frozen gases. Each of the planets has unique characteristics that make it different from the others.

Materials:
Metric tape measure or ruler
Calculator
Small posterboards or flags
Copy paper

Challenge Question: How much space would you need to create a model of the solar system?

Procedure:
1. On a blank sheet of paper, draw and label a picture of our solar system with the sun and nine planets. In your drawing, place the planets in relative position of their distance from the sun and each of the other planets.

2. You will now design a larger model of our solar system. This model might be done in your classroom, a hallway, the gymnasium, or the playground. To create a scale model of the solar system, one of the first things you have to determine is the amount of area in which you have to place your solar system. You must also decide with what units of measurement you will be working. In this activity, the sun-to-planet distances will be given in terms of millions of kilometers. It is suggested that you use meters for the measuring of the scale model. In the space on the next page, record the available distance you have to create the model of the solar system. Also determine the ratio of scale model distance to the actual distance of Pluto by dividing the available distance by the known sun-to-Pluto distance.

Name: _____ Date:_____

Inquiry Activity **9**: Scaling the Solar System (cont.)

Available distance for model (meters)	Sun-to-Pluto distance (million kilometers)	Scale Model Ratio (meters/million) kilometers)
_____	5,900	_____

3. Using the scale model ratio you found in the previous step, determine the sun-to-planet distances for the remaining planets of the solar system. Record the calculated distances for each planet in the chart below.

    Example: if the available distance for the model scale solar system is 86 meters, then Pluto would be located 86 meters from the sun, and Earth would be 2.19 meters from the sun.

    Scale Model ratio   =   86 meters divided by 5,900 million kilometers
                         =   0.0146 meters/million kilometers.

    Sun-to-Earth distance =   0.0146 meters/million kilometers x 150 million kilometers
                           =   2.19 meters

Exploration/Data Collection:

PLANET	Sun-to-Planet Distance (million kilometers)	X	Scale Model ratio	=	Sun-to-Planet scale distance
Sun					
Mercury	58				
Venus	108				
Earth	150				
Mars	228				
Jupiter	778				
Saturn	1,430				
Uranus	2,870				
Neptune	4,500				
Pluto	5,900				

71

Inquiry Activity 9: Scaling the Solar System (cont.)

4. Assign each planet to a group of students. Have the students in each group research facts about their assigned planet. Facts might include distance from sun; size of planet; average temperature of planet; length of planet's day; length of planet's year; etc. Have the group of students draw and color a poster listing the name of the planet and their interesting facts. (See sample below.)

5. Using the sun-to-planet scale distance, measure out the distance for each of the planets. Place a sign or flag with the planet's name at each of the planet locations. How does the larger scale model compare to the drawing you drew in Step 1?

    _____

    _____

    _____

6. The Asteroid Belt, a group of minor planets, is located about 445,000,000 kilometers from the sun. Place a sign or flag on your scale model locating the Asteroid Belt. In terms of the other planets, describe the location of the Asteroid Belt.

    _____

    _____

    _____

Name: _____ Date:_____

Inquiry Activity **9**: Scaling the Solar System (cont.)

Conclusions:

7. Generalize as to why the planet Earth is the only planet in the solar system that is known to have the capability to support life as we know it.

_____

_____

_____

_____

_____

Summary:

On completing this activity, the students should have an understanding of not only the vastness of the solar system but the realization that the first four planets, Venus, Mercury, Earth and Mars (sometimes called the Inner Planets), are located very close to the sun, while the remaining five planets are a great distance from the sun. Students should also recognize that the distance a planet is from the sun may be one of the prime reasons that the planet can or cannot support life.

Extensions:

Have each student select a planet, other than Earth, and create a travel brochure for reaching the planet. Information included in the brochure might be distance to the planet from the Earth, travel time to the planet, features of the planet that a traveler might observe, and things a traveler might do on the planet. The travel brochure might represent a mix of real and fictional activities. (An example might include a traveler to Mars skiing on the polar ice caps.)

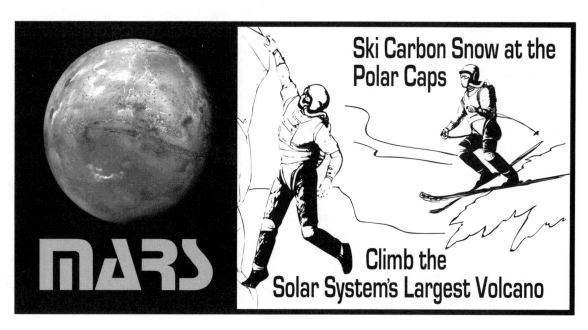

Name: _____   Date:_____

Inquiry Activity 9 : Scaling the Solar System (cont.)

Assessment:

1. Each student's drawing should show his/her understanding of the order of the planets and relative distances from each other. Accurate drawings will show the first four planets relatively close to the sun and each other. The remaining five planets will be found at much greater distances from the sun.

2-3. Each student's answer will vary for his/her solar system models depending on the amount of available space the student has to create the model.

4. Students' posters will vary.

5. Each student's answer will vary but may reflect the fact that all planets are not equal distance from each other. Student's reflections might also indicate the recognition that planets closer to the sun are more closely grouped than the planets that are farther from the sun.

6. Each student's answer should indicate that the Asteroid Belt is located in the region between Mars and Jupiter.

7. Each student's answer should recognize the fact that Earth is at a distance from the sun that allows it to be not too cold or too hot but just the right temperature to support life. Student's answer might also show an understanding that the location of the earth from the sun might be an acceptable distance to allow for the needed atmosphere to support life.

BIBLIOGRAPHY

Children's Literature Resources

Alfredson, H. and Ahlin, P. (1993). *The Night the Moon Came By.* This is a nighttime adventure full of fantasy and adventure by the light of the moon.

Asimov, I. (1988). *The Asteroids.* New York: Dell Yearling, Publishers. This is a book that includes information about the asteroids with a discussion about their status as planetoids and the possibilities for future exploration.

Asimov, I. (1988). *Comets and Meteors.* New York: Dell Yearling, Publishers. This is an informational book about "shooting stars" and their relationship to comets.

Asimov, I. (1988). *Did Comets Kill the Dinosaurs?* New York: Dell Yearling, Publishers. This is a description of the science behind the extinction of the dinosaurs and the possible causes, including facts about meteors and comets.

Branley, F. M. and Kelley, T. *Floating in Space.* This is a story of what it's like to explore space on the space shuttle. This is from a series entitled, *Let's-Read-and-Find-Out Science Series.*

Dash, J. & Petricic, D. (2000). *The Longitude Prize.* New York: Frances Foster Books, Farrar, Straus, and Giroux. The story of John Harrison, inventor of watches and clocks, who spent forty years working on a time machine that could be used to accurately determine longitude at sea.

Forey, P., and Fitzsimons, C. (1988). *An Instant Guide to Stars and Planets.* New York: Gramercy Books. This is a field guide with accurate up-to-date (1988) information. It includes guides to the solar system, the constellations, and the structure of the universe.

Gibbons, G. (1993). *The Planets.* New York: Holiday House. This book includes basic information supported by excellent illustrations on the characteristics of the nine planets.

Henner, B. and Ruhl, G. (1999). *First on the Moon.* This book details the *Apollo 11* mission to the moon and the exploration of the moon's Sea of Tranquility by Neil Armstrong and Buzz Aldrin. The book includes actual photos from NASA chronicling the mission. The book also includes a timeline of milestones in space exploration.

Hoffman, M. and Ray, J. illus. (1988) *Sun, Moon, and Stars.* This book shares over twenty myths and legends concerning the heavens. The stories represent many cultures from throughout the world and include sun lore, moon lore, and sky lore.

BIBLIOGRAPHY (CONT.)

The *Planet Library* Series includes a set of nine books that includes photographs, diagrams, and up-to-date information about members of our solar system. Historical background includes information about the discovery of each planet and the other members of the solar system.

Kerrod, R. (2000). *Asteroids, Comets, and Meteors*. Minneapolis, MN: Lerner Publications.

Kerrod, R. (2000). *Jupiter*. Minneapolis, MN: Lerner Publications.

Kerrod, R. (2000). *Mars*. Minneapolis, MN: Lerner Publications.

Kerrod, R. (2000). *Mercury and Venus*. Minneapolis, MN: Lerner Publications.

Kerrod, R. (2000). *The Moon*. Minneapolis, MN: Lerner Publications.

Kerrod, R. (2000). *Planet Earth*. Minneapolis, MN: Lerner Publications.

Kerrod, R. (2000). *Saturn*. Minneapolis, MN: Lerner Publications.

Kerrod, R. (2000). *The Sun*. Minneapolis, MN: Lerner Publications.

Kerrod, R. (2000). *Uranus, Neptune, and Pluto*. Minneapolis, MN: Lerner Publications.

Krupp, E.C. and Krupp, R.R. illus. (1993). *The Moon and You*. New York: Macmillan Publishing Co. Astronomer Dr. E.C. Krupp introduces us to the earth's nearest neighbor. He includes information about gravity, tides, the moon's phases, human lunar exploration, and moon mythology. The illustrations are excellent.

Leedy, L. (1993). *Postcards From Pluto: A Tour of the Solar System*. This book details an imaginary tour led by a robot. Students learn scientific facts about the nine planets, the asteroids, and the planet moons.

Mayall, R.N. and Mayall, M. and Wyckoff, J. (1985). *The Sky Observer's Guide: A Handbook for Amateur Astronomers*. New York: Golden Press. This is a beginning field guide that includes information about the moon, sun, planets, stars, comets, meteors, etc. It also includes information about becoming a sky observer and the equipment needed.

Ride, S. and O'Shaughnessy. T. (1999). *The Mystery of Mars*. New York: Crown Publishers. This is a book about NASA's *Pathfinder* mission to Mars and the decades of research on Earth's nearest planetary neighbor. Astronaut Sally Ride is the co-author.

Snowden, S. (1989). *The Young Astronomer, An Usborne Guide*. Tulsa, OK: EDC Publishing. This is an introductory book for beginners. It starts out with a discussion of the equipment needed to explore in space and includes background information in astronomy.

The *Out of This World* Series includes a set of four books that includes photographs, diagrams, and up-to-date information about Jupiter, Saturn, the sun, and Venus. Historical background includes information about the discovery of each planet and the other members of the solar system.

Spangenburg, R. and Moser, K. (2001). *A Look at Jupiter*. New York: Franklin Watts, A Division of Scholastic, Inc.

Bibliography (cont.)

Spangenburg, R. and Moser, K. (2001). *A Look at Saturn*. New York: Franklin Watts, A Division of Scholastic, Inc.

Spangenburg, R. and Moser, K. (2001). *A Look at the Sun*. New York: Franklin Watts, A Division of Scholastic, Inc.

Spangenburg, R. and Moser, K. (2001). *A Look at Venus*. New York: Franklin Watts, A Division of Scholastic, Inc.

Stott, C. (1998). *Out of This World*. Cambridge, MA: Candlewick Press. Carole Stott includes information about our expanding universe, measurement scales in astronomy, gravity, telescopes, lunar exploration, and space stations.

Tradin, D. B. (1999). *Is There Life on Mars?*. New York: Margaret K. McElderry Books of Simon & Schuster Publishers. This is a book that explores the historical speculation about life on Mars. It includes some of the more recent questions and information about Mars exploration.

VanCleave, J. (1991). *Astronomy for Every Kid*. New York: John Wiley and Sons. This book includes ideas and activities for school, science fairs, and fun in astronomy.

Yolen, J. and Schoenherr, J. (1987). *Owl Moon*. New York: Scholastic. This is an interesting story about a boy and his dad and their search for owls by the light of a winter full moon.

Web Resources

http://phys.udallas.edu/C3P/altconcp.html#Inertia

http://www.aspsky.org - Astronomical Society of the Pacific.

http://www.jpl.nasa.gov/galileo/ - This is the site for NASA's *Galileo* mission to Jupiter

http://www.seds.org/nineplanets/nineplanets/nineplanets.html - This site includes material on the nine planets and was created by students at the University of Arizona.

http://pds.jpl.nasa.gov/planets/ - A tour of the solar system created by NASA

Software

Beyond Planet Earth, by Discovery Channel School. This CD-ROM includes an interactive journey through our solar system utilizing video footage and still photographs.

Smallberg, R., Siletti, W.L., Laspisa, C. (1995). *A Field Trip to The Sky,* Pleasantville, N.Y.: Sunburst Communications, Inc. This CD-ROM includes a field trip with varying perspectives on the relationship of the sun, Earth, and moon.

BIBLIOGRAPHY (CONT.)

Curriculum Resources

Beals, K., Erickson, J., and Sneider, C.I. (2000). *Messages From Space: The Solar System and Beyond.* Great Explorations in Math and Science (GEMS). Berkeley, CA.: Lawrence Hall of Science, University of California. This exciting teaching unit opens with a binary-coded message "from space" and takes the class on a journey through our solar system and beyond. Students model size and distance, explore how systems may have formed, ponder stellar "life zones," and design space travel brochures.

Caduto, M.J. and Bruchac, J. (1988). *Keepers of the Earth: Native American Stories and Environmental Education Activities for Children.* Golden, CO: Fulcrum Press. This is an unusual curriculum source in that it deals with the culture and heritage of early Americans. The book features Native American stories, myths, and legends concerning the earth. Each story is accompanied by environmental education activities. The activities specifically dealing with astronomy include: *How Grandmother Spider Stole the Sun, How Raven Made the Tides, How Coyote Was the Moon,* and *How Fisher Went to the Skyland: The Origin of the Big Dipper.*

Caduto, M.J. and Bruchac, J. (1994). *Keepers of the Night: Native American Stories and Environmental Education Activities for Children.* Golden, CO: Fulcrum Press. This is another book in the series by Caduto and Bruchac that includes Native American stories, myths, and legends. The two stories that are related specifically to astronomy are *Oot-Kwah-Tah, The Seven Star Dancers,* and *The Creation of the Moon.*

Glaser, D., Beals, K., Pompea, S., and Willard, C. (2003). *Living with a Star.* Great Explorations in Math and Science (GEMS). Berkeley, CA: Lawrence Hall of Science, University of California. This unit deals with the sun and our relationship to our primary source of energy on Earth. It includes experiments with ultraviolet light and information about space weather. It includes a NASA-sponsored unit on electromagnetic energy and solar particles on Earth. CD-ROM included.

Gould, A., Willard, C., and Pompea, S. (2000). *The Real Reason for the Seasons: Sun-Earth Connections.* Great Explorations in Math and Science (GEMS). Berkeley, CA.: Lawrence Hall of Science, University of California. Sponsored by NASA and carefully developed to help students overcome persistent misconceptions about the causes of the seasons, this unit features modeling and hands-on activities. Includes a CD-ROM with a wide selection of photographs, films, websites, simulations, and software.

Grossman, M.C., Shapiro, I.I., and Ward, R.B. (1997). Project Aries (Astronomy Resources for Intercurricular Elementary Science) *Module Two: Astronomy I: Thinking About the Earth and the Sun.* Cambridge, MA: Harvard University. Reference for the Sun Location Measurement Device (SLMD) constructed and used in Student Inquiry Activity 6.

Sneider, C.I. (1986). *Earth, Moon, and Stars.* Great Explorations in Math and Science (GEMS). Berkeley, CA.: Lawrence Hall of Science, University of California. Students learn a great deal about the earth and astronomy with modeling and observation activities that focus on gravity, the shape of our planet, moon phases, eclipses, and the stars. A questionnaire on the earth's shape and gravity makes an excellent pre- and post-assessment tool.

Sutter, D., Sneider, C.I., Gould, A., Willard, C., and DeVore, E. (1993). *Moons of Jupiter.* Great Explorations in Math and Science (GEMS). Berkeley, CA.: Lawrence Hall of Science, University of California. Observing and recording moon orbits over time, students replicate Galileo's historic telescopic study of Jupiter's moons and learn why his observations contributed to the birth of modern astronomy. Students experiment with craters, create scale models, and take a tour of the Jupiter system.